MASTERPIECES
OF
BIBLICAL ART

MASTERPIECES
OF
BIBLICAL ART

MASTERPIECES OF BIBLICAL ART

Catholic Digest Edition
College of St. Thomas
St. Paul, Minnesota

The Catholic Press
Chicago

1973

CONTENTS

THE ARTISTS

FOREWORD

*M*asterpieces of Biblical Art is a collection of outstanding religious paintings of the Western World from the period beginning in the thirteenth century, on the eve of the Renaissance, and extending into the nineteenth century. Ninety-five biblical themes are illustrated, arranged in the order in which the subjects appear in the Bible.

Each reproduction is accompanied by an appropriate passage from the Bible, a commentary on the artist's intentions in the picture, and a statement of the artist's significance in the history of art. In addition, the reader will find assistance in the following notes, which list the artists chronologically, from Giotto di Bondone in the thirteenth century to Camille Corot in the nineteenth.

THE ITALIAN PRIMITIVES

A glorious era in biblical art begins with the great Italian primitives of the thirteenth and fourteenth centuries, who brought to painting a new spirit and new techniques. The term *primitive* is not applied to them in the sense of unschooled or erratic; they are discoverers, pioneers, innovators.

Giotto di Bondone (1266?-1337), the earliest of the primitives in this collection, is noted principally for his frescoes in the Arena (or Scrovegni) Chapel in Padua (58, 73, 77, 86).* He used pieces of sculpture for his models and ended the two-dimensional era in Italian art, producing solid, rounded figures. A more significant innovation was his realistic depiction of emotion, particularly striking in his *The Lamentation Over Christ* (86). The angels and mourners around the body of Christ are arranged according to the canons of Byzantine painting, but the profound grief they are shown as expressing is without precedent in biblical painting.

Duccio di Buoninsegna (c. 1255-1319) is known for a single great work, a *Maestà* ("Majesty of the Virgin"), painted as an altarpiece for the cathedral in his native Siena. Both the front and the reverse of the altar-

---
*Numbers refer to paintings in this volume.

piece were covered with paintings; the front was devoted to events in the life of Mary, the reverse to forty-four scenes from the life of Christ, of which the pictures reproduced here (63, 65, 69) were once a part. The *Maestà* was regarded as one of the glories of Siena, and its installation in the cathedral, on June 9, 1311, was an occasion for a festive procession. Two centuries later, it was removed and replaced by a large bronze tabernacle. Not until the nineteenth century was Duccio recognized as one of the greatest painters of the early Renaissance.

Simone Martini (1285?-1344) was, like Duccio, a native of Siena, and he succeeded him as leader of the Sienese School. His *Christ Carrying the Cross* (81) includes both biblical and traditional elements. Simon of Cyrene helps to carry the Cross, while the women with upraised arms are probably intended to represent the Virgin and Veronica. Noted especially for the variety of his portraiture, Martini has here emphasized the derisive attitude of many of those in the scene.

The Three Marys at the Tomb (89), one of a group of paintings made for San Piero Maggiore in Florence about 1371, is commonly attributed to a Florentine artist, Andrea Orcagna (1308-1376), or to Jacopo Cione. The treatment of figures in the painting recalls that of Giotto, who is said to have been Orcagna's teacher.

The Adoration of the Magi (56) is one of the few surviving works of Gentile da Fabriano (c. 1370-1427), founder of an Umbrian School of painting. His style is rich and elaborate, full of intimate details of costume and furniture in the courts of northern Italy; it is similar to the style of his contemporary Lochner in Germany and the Limbourgs in France, and is known as "International Gothic." In the arches of the cornice, Fabriano has added imaginative pictures of the Journey of the Magi, while the base, or gradine, includes paintings of the Nativity, the Flight into Egypt, and the Presentation in the Temple.

The last of the Italian primitives in the collection is Giovanni di Paolo (c. 1403-1482/83), a Sienese. His *The Head of the Baptist Is Brought Before Herod* (68) is one of a series of panels illustrating the life of St. John. The court atmosphere and the concern with detail recall Fabriano, but Giovanni's is a decidedly different talent. Note the dual illustration of Salome's page, bringing in the head of the Baptist (at right) and finally presenting it to Herod. with a towel under the still-haloed trophy on its salver.

THE NORTHERN PRIMITIVES

In the northern countries—in France, Germany, Holland, and Flanders— there were circles of artists who had fruitful contacts with the new art of Italy, and who, in turn, often contributed something new to the complex of influences in the art world of the Renaissance.

The first of the German primitives is Master Bertram (1370-1410), who worked in northern Germany (mainly Hamburg) toward the end of the fourteenth century. A notable feature of his art was the use of contemporary costume in his biblical scenes, as in *Cain Slaying Abel* (4). The weapon used by Cain appears to be the jawbone of an ass, probably suggested by its use in the story of Samson (Judges 15:14).

Jean Fouquet (c. 1420-1481), a French primitive, is noted as the brilliant founder of the French school of portraiture, but his genius is most apparent in his miniatures, such as *The Fall of Jericho* (29), painted to illustrate a manuscript of the *Jewish Antiquities* of Flavius Josephus. Fouquet spent a fruitful apprenticeship at Bourges, where he may have known the Limbourgs, who were likewise masters of the miniature.

The Annunciation (52), by Rogier van der Weyden (1399/1400-1464), illustrates the draftsmanship and coloring skill of this early Flemish master as well as his attention to traditional details—the prayer book held by the Virgin, the sconce, chandelier, and the vase of lilies, all tokens of Mary's virtue. *The Entombment* (87) exemplifies van der Weyden's restraint in portraying scenes of intense emotion. Hans Memling (c. 1433-1494), a pupil of van der Weyden, attempted a similar serenity in his portraiture. In his *Presentation of the Christ Child in the Temple* (57), the people are all realistically portrayed but seem preoccupied with their thoughts, perhaps contemplating Simeon's ominous prophecy (Luke 2:35). This curious tranquillity is apparent in many of the great paintings of the Golden Age of Flemish art; it is especially remarkable in *The Marriage at Cana* (64), by Gerard David (1450/60-1523), which conveys a feeling of gentle suspense in spite of the activity of the servants in the foreground.

Dieric Bouts (c. 1415-1475) was born in Holland and worked for some years in Haarlem. However, his most important paintings were produced in Louvain, where he settled in 1449 and where he was made official painter in 1468. He is represented here only by Old Testament paintings (8, 20, 22, 24, and 40); four of these, however—all except number 20—were painted for a retable of the Blessed Sacrament and include elements understood to prefigure the Eucharist—the bread and wine offered by Melchizedek, the Passover lamb, the manna, and the food brought by an angel to Elijah.

The last of the northern primitives in the collection is Geertgen tot Sint Jans (c. 1465-1490/95), the first painter of note whose entire productive career was spent in the city of Haarlem. In his *The Raising of Lazarus* (72), he closely followed a painting of the subject by his master, Albert van Ouwater. As in Ouwater's picture, there are Scribes and Pharisees present, identified by their traditional emblems: the Scribe holds his writing implements, the Pharisee a case with a scroll.

THE ITALIAN RENAISSANCE

The Renaissance in Italian art is commonly regarded as consisting of two principal eras: an Early Renaissance, comprising most of the fifteenth century, and a High Renaissance, extending to the closing years of the sixteenth.

The fifteenth century was a time of ripening and development. The great event of the Early Renaissance was the emergence of Masaccio (1401-1428). His career lasted only a few years, but the technical skills he developed and the directness and emotional honesty of his work had an enduring impact on the art of the Western World. In his own day, his paintings in the Brancacci Chapel in Florence (70) were being carefully studied by other artists, and in modern times painters are still seeking a deeper understanding of their art by studying Masaccio.

Following Masaccio comes a long series of master painters, many of whom were unexcelled in their special competence: Piero della Francesca, Castagno, Verrocchio, Botticelli, Mantegna.

Piero della Francesca (1415/20-1492) won his fame through his portraits and decorative work for the *condottiere* Federico da Montefeltro and other art-loving war lords of his day. He was a master of perspective, as may be seen from his *Solomon and the Queen of Sheba* (39) and *The Nativity* (54), and in his last years he composed a treatise on the subject.

Andrea del Castagno (c. 1423-1457) was, like Masaccio, a brilliant, short-lived genius who left a rich heritage for the world of art. A celebrated item in that legacy is his *The Youthful David* (35), painted on leather, for use as a decorative shield on festive occasions.

Andrea Verrocchio (c. 1435-1498) achieved his greatest fame as a teacher of Leonardo, Perugino, and Ghirlandaio. He was primarily a sculptor, and his skill as a painter in known through only a few examples, one of which is his *The Baptism of Christ* (62). Leonardo collaborated on several parts of this work, notably in painting one of the angels.

Sandro Botticelli (c. 1445-1510) was esteemed as *the* painter of grace and beauty, and his studio was one of the busiest in Italy. He was also a painter of somber scenes, such as *Mordecai Lamenting Before the Gates of the Palace* (43). Once thought to represent Vashti after her repudiation by Ahasuerus (Esther 1:10-22), the picture is now believed to illustrate Mordecai's grief on hearing of a decree against the Jews (Esther 4:1).

In an age when Italian artists all seemed drawn to Florence, Andrea Mantegna (1431-1506) found his opportunities in northern cities, though he was influenced by the Florentine School. While respectful of traditions, he was an innovator in his use of realism in dramatic episodes. *The Ascension* (92) boldly depicts the event, showing Christ rising on what appears to be a small cloud; he is surrounded by miniature cherubs and carries the traditional banner of the Resurrection. The witnesses look up with frank amazement.

The High Renaissance is an era of perfect maturity. It is a period marked by openness and freedom in philosophy and literature, by great technical mastery, and by the advent of three great artists—Leonardo, Michelangelo, and Raphael.

Acknowledged as the greatest painter of the Renaissance, Leonardo da Vinci (1452-1519) was also an accomplished sculptor, goldsmith, engraver, architect, and engineer, and he had demonstrated his command of most of these skills by the time he was thirty. *The Last Supper* (75), his best-known religious painting, depicts the confusion of the apostles on hearing Christ say that one of them is about to betray him (Matthew 26:21-23). A fresco in the refectory of Santa Mario delle Grazie in Milan, the painting was suffering from moisture damage as early as 1545 and has continued to deteriorate in spite of all efforts to check and repair the damage. However, the picture will always be regarded with a kind of mystic reverence, as one of the greatest works of religious art.

At the opening of the sixteenth century, the prestige of Michelangelo (1475-1564) equaled that of Leonardo. He was somewhat less profound, a little less versatile, but he was aggressive and dynamic in promoting his own great talent. His works reproduced in this collection (1, 2, 45) are from his frescoes for the ceiling of the Sistine Chapel in the Vatican, painted between 1508 and 1512. He was by choice a monumental sculptor, and here, as in all his paintings, the figures are the dominant elements.

Raphael Sanzio (1483-1520), who could challenge Michelangelo in popularity, came to Florence in 1504 after four years in the studio of Perugino in Rome. His *The Marriage of the Virgin* (51), painted at that time, depicts a scene from the apocryphal Gospel of James. Joseph holds a flowering rod, a sign of his election; around him are the rejected suitors with barren rods. One, in frustration, breaks his rod across his knee. *The Vision of Ezekiel* (46), painted twelve years later, toward the end of Raphael's brief career, attempts to picture the Lord attended by the cherubim and "living creatures" (Ezekiel 1:4—5:10).

Among the many followers of Leonardo, one of the most prolific was the Lombard painter Bernardo Luini (1480/85-1532). Clever, inventive, imaginative, his works (6, 21, 23) suggest to some critics what Leonardo might have been if his talents had been differently applied. Andrea del Sarto (1486-1530) also was drawn to imitate Leonardo, though Raphael and Michelangelo were also major influences in his work. A small but promising talent of the era was Mariotto Albertinelli (1474-1515), remembered for the beauty of a single work, his *The Visitation* (53).

In the last half of the sixteenth century, three Venetian masters dominated Italian art—Titian (1477?-1576), Tintoretto (1518-1594), and Paolo Veronese (1528-1588). Titian came from the Venetian workshops of the Bellinis to begin his long career of over seventy years in the service of Pope Paul III, Charles V, Philip II, and many other prelates and princes. Called the "perfect painter," he was equally successful with themes from Scripture, legend, and mythology, and retained his individuality as others yielded to the tides of change. In *The Fall of Man* (3), he utilized his artistic skills while disposing of, in a simple manner, problems of illustrating the Bible text: Eve plucks a fruit from the tree and Adam waits to receive the fateful gift. The Tree was most commonly pictured as a fig, but artists often found other fruits more attractive. Titian shows two trees—a fig and a peach; a cherubic serpent tenders the fruit to Eve, and Adam reaches out uncertainly, as if to stop her. *Noli Me Tangere* (90) illustrates another garden scene, the encounter of Christ and Mary Magdalene after the Resurrection (John 20:17). Both pictures were painted when the artist was more than ninety years old.

The second great Venetian in this collection—Tintoretto (Jacopo Robusti)—spent a brief apprenticeship (ten days, some say) with Titian, then opened his own studio, and claimed to offer art with the draftsmanship of Michelangelo and the color of Titian. The great treasury of his work is the Scuola di San Rocco in Venice, which he decorated with fifty-six majestic frescoes, painted over a period of twenty-three years (1564-1587). This is the source of his *Christ Before Pilate* (79). Jesus awaits the sentence, but Pilate washes his hands and proclaims his own innocence, leaving the decision to the crowd of spectators. In the right foreground, the court scribe has halted in his transcription.

The last of the Venetian masters in the collection is Paolo Caliari, known as Veronese. He was a magician in his handling of light, which warms and animates all his work. Another talent of Veronese was his ability to paint luxurious costumes—sometimes distractingly prominent, as in his *Moses Saved from the Nile* (19). His *Calvary* (83) presents another characteristic of his religious art—his tendency to introduce figures and action unknown in traditional renderings; for example, the grief of Mary Magdalene (at the foot of the Cross), the swooning Virgin (center foreground), and the workmen and draft horse (brought to take down Christ's body) are conventional elements, but usually not brought together in the same scene, and the mysterious veiled figure at the right is a sheer invention of the artist. Similarly, in a *Last Supper*, Veronese included a buffoon, waiters, and numerous unidentified guests. When the Inquisition condemned these innovations, the painter replied by simply changing his title to *Dinner in the House of Levi*, a supper scene in which the force of tradition was less important.

THE CENTURY OF THE BAROQUE

At the close of the sixteenth century, a new style appeared in the art and architecture of Europe. The new style came to be called baroque from the Portuguese word *barroco* ("odd," "irregular"). In painting, it was marked by distortion of the figure, an expansive composition, and a new use of contrasts of light and dark (*chiaroscuro*), mainly for the purpose of dramatic effects.

While art history assigns the baroque era to the seventeenth century, many of the baroque characteristics are found in sixteenth-century painting. The Dutch artist Hieronymous Bosch (1450/60-1516), obsessed with the bizarre and grotesque, is usually classed as baroque. His painting *The Crowning with Thorns* (80) shows his curious use of savage symbols. A famous follower of Bosch, Pieter Bruegel the Elder (1528/30-1659), displays some baroque traits in his grandiose *The Tower of Babel* (7). And in Spain, the genius of El Greco (1541-1614) found expression in a style that is baroque in many respects (55, 74, 76, 82, 85, 88, 93). Typical of the Spanish baroque is *Joseph Thrown into the Pit* (16), by Bartolomé Esteban Murillo (1618-1682).

In Italy, Caravaggio (1573-1610) imposed a vogue for baroque chiaroscuro effects through his brilliant use of this technique in such pictures as *The Calling of Matthew* (67) and *The Conversion of Paul* (95). Other masterpieces of Italian baroque were *Jacob's Dream* (14) by Domenico Feti (1589-1624); *Saul and the Witch of Endor* (37) by Salvator Rosa (1615-1675); *The Sacrifice of Noah* (5) by Bernardo Cavallino (1622-1654); *The Twelve-Year-Old Christ Among the Doctors* (61) by Luca Giordano (1632-1705); and *Jacob Receiving the Bloodstained Coat of Joseph* (17) by an unknown Italian master of the seventeenth century.

In the North, the most gifted of the baroque artists was Peter Paul Rubens (1577-1640). His studio in Antwerp was a veritable factory, with apprentices and aides working under the master's supervision to supply paintings commissioned from various countries. His paintings (31, 38, 41, 42, 50) exhibit an almost unparalleled virtuosity and an apparent relish for challenging subjects.

A Flemish painter, David Teniers the Elder (1582-1649), and two Dutchmen, Gerbrandt van den Eeckhout (1621-1674) and Jan Steen (1626-1679), are the final artists in this brief survey of the baroque. Teniers'

Daniel in the Lions' Den (48) reflects the influence of Rubens, in whose studio Teniers worked. The prophet, in the background of the picture, expresses his thanks (Daniel 6:22). Van den Eeckhout and Steen are skillful genre painters, but the anachronisms in their works (13, 44) are distracting.

SOME INDEPENDENTS

Albrecht Dürer (1471-1528), regarded as Germany's greatest artist, brought German painting from the Gothic Age into the Renaissance. He was in touch with the Italian masters, such as Raphael, and made two trips to Italy and a journey to the Netherlands, where he met Erasmus and studied the Dutch portraitists. Portraiture was perhaps his supreme talent, expressed in his painting known as *The Four Apostles* (94), which is considered to be the artist's finest work.

Rembrandt van Rijn (1606-1669), foremost of the Dutch masters and one of the greatest artists of all time, is perhaps the supreme biblical illustrator, having used Scripture subjects in a major part of his vast production—which included more than 600 paintings and 300 etchings. Trained under a classic master—Lastman—Rembrandt himself was never committed to any school. Much of his work, however, is remarkable for a characteristic lighting which can be called baroque. This lighting is an important element in practically all of the Rembrandt paintings reproduced here (10, 15, 18, 26, 28, 30, 32, 34, 36, 37, 49, 66, 71, 78, 84, 91).

Georges de la Tour (1593-1652), a French provincial artist, painted many candlelit night scenes such as *Joseph the Carpenter* (60). He was rediscovered by art historians in 1915, his works previously having been assigned, rather uncertainly, to other masters. Baroque in the startling chiaroscuro of his painting, he was a classic realist in other respects.

Like La Tour, Nicolas Poussin (1594-1665) was born in a small provincial town in France, but he spent most of his creative career in Rome. His pictures, about equally divided between biblical and mythological subjects, are painted in a style in which he attempted to emulate the composition and draftsmanship of Raphael and the color and vigor of Titian (12, 25, 27, 33, 59).

The Destruction of Sodom (9) is one of a number of biblical scenes painted early in his career by Camille Corot (1796-1875), primarily known as a landscape painter. The picture was rejected by the Paris Salon of 1843, but critics now see in these early works of Corot the freshness and directness which have become the ideal values of modern landscape painting.

1. MICHELANGELO: *God Creating the Sun*

2. MICHELANGELO: *God Creating Adam*

< OPPOSITE PAGE EIGHTEEN

1. God Creating the Sun (detail)

BY MICHELANGELO 1475–1564 *Italian School*

Sistine Chapel, Vatican, Rome

God made the two great lights, the greater light to rule the day and the smaller one to rule the night, and he made the stars. GENESIS 1:16

MICHELANGELO'S CONTEMPORARIES described the special quality of his works with the word *terribilità,* which can best be translated as "awesomeness." The figure of God in *God Creating the Sun* has all the power of some mighty upheaval in nature: the swirling movement of the body and its draperies spirals headlong like the rush of a tornado. Unlike the random whirlwind, however, the force that we see here is creative; it seems to gather to a point in the Lord's right hand, which literally scoops the new star out of space (the lower curve of the orb may be found in the upper left-hand corner of our picture).

< PRECEDING PAGE

2. God Creating Adam (detail)

BY MICHELANGELO 1475–1564 *Italian School*

Sistine Chapel, Vatican, Rome

Then the Lord God formed man out of the dust of the ground and breathed into his nostrils the breath of life, and man became a living being. GENESIS 2:7

SURGING FORWARD accompanied by a host of angels, God stretches forth His life-giving hand to the newly created Adam, whose hand stirring in its first gesture may be seen at the left of our picture. With His left arm the Lord shelters Eve, as yet unborn. Though still a spirit among the other spirits in His cloud cloak, she peers half curious, half frightened, at her future spouse with whom she is already linked through God's embrace.

3. TITIAN: *The Fall of Man*

< PRECEDING PAGE

3. The Fall of Man

BY TITIAN 1477?–1576 *Italian School*

The Prado, Madrid

She took of its fruit and ate it, and also gave some to her husband and he ate. GENESIS 3:6

BOTH TITIAN AND MICHELANGELO belonged to the period in art known as the High Renaissance and shared a belief in the essential dignity of man. Titian, however, was less exclusively preoccupied with man himself than was Michelangelo; through his interest in landscape and the misty atmosphere that envelops it in his native Venice, he came to see the world in terms of shimmering color rather than solid form. There is, to be sure, no lack of human drama in this scene with its recoiling Adam and yearning Eve, but it is rendered more poignant by the golden vista of that Garden which they are about to forfeit, stretching out behind them till it melts into the sky. In this benign atmosphere even the serpent peering down amid the foliage looks more like a mischievous cupid than the incarnation of evil; only his forked tail, hard to distinguish from the branches, reveals the evil end that is so playfully masked by a winsome beginning.

4. MASTER BERTRAM: *Cain Slaying Abel*

< PRECEDING PAGE

4. Cain Slaying Abel (panel from the Grabow Altar)
BY MASTER BERTRAM C.1370–1410 *German School*
Kunsthalle, Hamburg

Cain said to his brother Abel, "Let us go out into the field." Now when they were in the field, Cain turned against his brother Abel and slew him. GENESIS 4:8

THE STRIKING NEW REALISM of the Italian Renaissance is perhaps best appreciated if we compare it with this picture, painted in the north of Europe more than a century before Michelangelo and Titian. Whereas the great Italian masters surround their figures with a strikingly real space, Master Bertram's scene takes place in the land of the imagination, where the sky is a flat expanse of gold. Silhouetted against it, Cain stands ready to deliver the fatal blow, but somehow we feel that it will never descend. Where the Italian Renaissance, with its drama and realism, exhorts us to see it now, Medieval art, by placing less stress on immediate action and emotional content, bids us to see it forever.

5. BERNARDO CAVALLINO: *The Sacrifice of Noe*

< PRECEDING PAGE

5. The Sacrifice of Noe

BY BERNARDO CAVALLINO 1622–1654 *Italian School*

Museum of Fine Arts of Houston, Texas
(Samuel H. Kress Collection)

Then Noe built an altar to the Lord; he took of every clean animal and of every clean bird, and offered holocausts on the altar. GENESIS 8:20

THE BAROQUE STYLE, which began with the seventeenth century in Italy, brings a heightening of dramatic expression that often verges on the theatrical. Comparing this picture with the tremendously vehement gestures found in Michelangelo's work, we are aware of something resembling a posed quality here. We might, in the long run, grow tired of looking at this group of actors, but there is no doubt that they convey the tale very well. The seventeenth century found a new concern with bringing the Scriptures to the understanding of a wide audience, and as a result, such explanatory pictures were much in demand.

6. BERNARDINO LUINI: *The Drunkenness of Noe*

< PRECEDING PAGE

6. The Drunkenness of Noe

BY BERNARDINO LUINI 1480/85–1532 *Italian School*
Brera Gallery, Milan

When he drank of the wine, he became drunk. . . . Ham
[the father of Chanaan] saw his father's nakedness and told
his two brothers outside. GENESIS 9:21–22

THIS NORTH ITALIAN ARTIST was a pupil of Leonardo da
Vinci, and if we look attentively we will find some likeness between the faces of the two sons who support Noe
and some of the disciples in plate 75. The landscape with
its infinite view, bisected by the grape "tree," will recall
Titian's background in the *Fall of Man,* while in the derisive expression of the third son we detect something more
akin to Northern painting (such as the *Crowning of*
Thorns by Bosch, plate 80). All of these influences have
a part in the North Italian school of painting, and as a sum-
ming up, the picture could hardly be more instructive.

7.   BRUEGEL THE ELDER: *The Tower of Babel*

< PRECEDING PAGE

7. The Tower of Babel

BY PIETER BRUEGEL THE ELDER, 1528/30–1569

Flemish School, Kunsthistorisches Museum, Vienna

"Let us build ourselves a city and a tower with its top in the heavens; let us make a name for ourselves lest we be scattered all over the earth." GENESIS 11:4

BRUEGEL, WHO LIVED in the Low Countries (today, Belgium and Holland), learned a great deal about how to organize a picture from the Italians; nevertheless, he remained true to his North European background in his love of fine detail, a heritage from the great tradition of Medieval manuscript illumination. In his background, he takes pains to show us every tree and every rooftop, however minute; while the foreground tells us the Bible story in terms of a complete review of building practices in a sixteenth-century town.

8.   DIERIC BOUTS: *Abraham and Melchisedec*

< PRECEDING PAGE

8. Abraham and Melchisedec
BY DIERIC BOUTS c.1415–1475 *Flemish School*
S. Pierre, Louvain, Belgium

Then Melchisedec, the king of Salem, brought out bread and wine; for he was a priest of the Most High God. He blessed Abram and said, "Blessed be Abram by the Most High God, creator of heaven and earth." GENESIS 14:18–19

FIFTEENTH-CENTURY FLEMISH PAINTING, too, experienced a renaissance, though it did not follow the same paths as the Early Renaissance in Italy. Where a painter like Masaccio strove for the greatest degree of concentration, both in composition and expression, Flemish painting strikes us as being more spread-out. Here we find less stress placed on the correct rendering of the human figure —indeed, Bouts's personages strike us as being rather stiff and weightless under their elaborate costumes. But they are far advanced in realism as compared to the cutout silhouettes of Master Bertram, painted a mere eighty years earlier, and what realism may be lacking in the bodies is compensated for in the highly individual faces. Some of these are actual portraits, like the man at the extreme left; others are types, such as the two central figures. However, even for the latter, Bouts must have made a study of actual Jewish faces, in order to lend a touch of authenticity to his scenes of the Old Testament.

9. COROT: *The Destruction of Sodom*

< PRECEDING PAGE

9. The Destruction of Sodom

BY CAMILLE COROT 1796–1875 *French School*

The Metropolitan Museum of Art, New York (Bequest
  of Mrs. H. O. Havemeyer, 1929, H. O. Havemeyer
  Collection)

*The Lord poured down on Sodom and Gomorra sulphur
and fire from the Lord out of heaven. He overthrew those
cities and the whole region, all the inhabitants of the cities
and the plants of the soil. But his wife who was behind him
looked back, and became a pillar of salt.* GENESIS 19:24–26

IN THIS PICTURE, as in many of the paintings by Poussin
which we shall come to presently, we are aware of a certain sense of restraint which is the hallmark of French
Classicism. Even in such a subject as this, fraught with
possibilities of violent drama and lurid background effects,
Corot's prevailing mood is one of resigned lamentation,
rather than of fright or despair. The worst has already
taken place: the city, no longer ablaze, has been reduced
to smoke-shrouded ruins. In the foreground Lot and his
daughters are led forth by the angel as if they were dazed
children. Even the figure of Lot's wife seems to have
turned back to gaze upon the destroyed city in quiet contemplation, not with the yearning or horror that one might
expect. By playing down human passions, Corot was better able to create a mood of pervasive sadness which
stands above the haphazard gusts of the emotions.

10. REMBRANDT: *The Dismissal of Agar*

< PRECEDING PAGE

10. The Dismissal of Agar

BY REMBRANDT 1606–1669 *Dutch School*

Victoria and Albert Museum, London

*Abraham rose early in the morning, took bread and a bottle
of water, and gave them to Agar, placing them on her shoul-
der. Then he dismissed her with the child.* GENESIS 21:14

THE POIGNANT PSYCHOLOGICAL INSIGHT which was the
great achievement of this great Dutch master's later years
(see, for example, *David Playing the Harp Before Saul,*
plate 36) is not yet fully present in this picture, dating
from the middle of his career; yet, we have only to compare it with the preceding plate by Corot to recognize his
bent. Here we do not find that equal stress on all parts of
the picture for the sake of a harmonious whole; instead, we
are immediately impelled to focus on the group of figures,
which, unlike Cavallino's nearly contemporary actors (see
the *Sacrifice of Noe,* plate 5), hold our interest by under-
playing rather than overplaying their roles. Only Ismael,
tugging at the bridle of the reluctant ass, gives a revealing
hint of the cruel and surprising situation. Agar—richly
clothed in the garments of a harem favorite as Rembrandt
imagined them—turns toward Abraham in bewildered
reproach; but her hand on the pommel reaches toward
the all-important water flask, symbol of her coming ordeal
and miraculous deliverance.

11. ANDREA DEL SARTO: *The Sacrifice of Abraham*

< PRECEDING PAGE

11. The Sacrifice of Abraham
BY ANDREA DEL SARTO 1486–1530 *Italian School*
The Cleveland Museum of Art (Holden Collection)

But an angel of the Lord called to him from heaven. . . .
He said, "Do not lay a hand on the boy." GENESIS 22:11–12

ANDREA DEL SARTO WAS ONE OF THAT GENERATION of
Florentine painters who followed in the wake—one might
almost say in the shadow—of Michelangelo. Unable to
help themselves from falling under the spell of his genius,
they found it difficult to discover any new direction which
he had not already explored in the style that was his crea-
tion. The hesitancy experienced by these men in matters of
art had a counterpart in the history of Florence itself:
greatest among the Italian city-states for nearly a century,
it had begun to slip from its position of pre-eminence. At
times, however, this mood of doubt has a special effective-
ness: in this story where the feelings of the boy are of fear
and bewilderment, Del Sarto paints him with a subtle
sympathy which might have escaped the dynamic Michelangelo. Unlike the Michelangelo figure of which the Isaac
is a copy, this boy does not seem about to burst his bonds,
but with panting breath he awaits his fate—fearful, yet
not without dignity.

12. POUSSIN: *Rebecca and Eliezer*

< PRECEDING PAGE

12. Rebecca and Eliezer

BY NICOLAS POUSSIN 1594–1665 *French School*

The Louvre, Paris

The servant hastened to meet her and said, "If you please, let me drink a little water from your jar." She answered, "Drink, sir." GENESIS 24:17–18

HERE, AS IN BOUTS'S *Abraham and Melchisedec* (plate 8), we have a scene of strangers meeting, and the comparison is an interesting one. At first we will be struck by the differences, rather than any similarity; for Poussin, though originally from the north of France, spent almost his entire career in Rome. There he absorbed the lessons of Renaissance art, and fell in love with the works of ancient Rome; indeed, he became the founder of a Classical school of French art whose continuation can be followed through to the nineteenth century (see Corot, plate 9). Despite his debt to the Mediterranean world, both of his own day and of the distant past, we have only to glance at the kind of pictures that the native Italians of that time were painting (see Cavallino, plate 5) in order to realize that his deliberate restraint of motion and emotion still, after a lapse of two centuries, bears some kinship to the understressed figures of Bouts's painting. It is interesting, too, that in writing about his *Rebecca and Eliezer* to a friend, Poussin says that he was especially interested in depicting the reactions of the bystanders as reflected in their countenances; an echo, however distant, of Bouts's stress on faces and their individual characteristics.

13. VAN DEN EECKHOUT: *Isaac Blessing Jacob*

< PRECEDING PAGE

13. Isaac Blessing Jacob

BY GERBRANDT VAN DEN EECKHOUT 1621–1674

Dutch School, The Metropolitan Museum of Art, New
   York (Bequest of Collis P. Huntington, 1925)

*Jacob went close to his father; Isaac touched him and said,
"The voice is the voice of Jacob, but the hands are the
hands of Esau." (He did not recognize him because his
hands were hairy like those of his brother Esau; so he
blessed him.)* GENESIS 27:22–23

WE WILL HAVE NO TROUBLE in immediately recognizing
the relatedness of this picture and Rembrandt's *Dismissal
of Agar* (plate 10). The spotlighting of a group of small
figures against a dark, rather mysterious background is
something that Van den Eeckhout learned from his great
teacher. Other influences must also have played a part in
his training: on the pretext of showing us the offering that
Jacob had brought to his blind father, the artist has intro-
duced a table into the foreground, richly decked with a
heavy carpet and precious vessels. A whole school of
painting in seventeenth-century Holland was devoted to sat-
isfying the demand for this kind of picture, called *still life*.

14.　DOMENICO FETI: *Jacob's Dream*

< PRECEDING PAGE

14. Jacob's Dream

BY DOMENICO FETI 1589–1624 *Italian School*

Kunsthistorisches Museum, Vienna

He dreamed that a ladder was set up on the ground with its top reaching to heaven; angels of God were ascending and descending on it. GENESIS 28:12

DIFFERENT AS THIS ITALIAN PICTURE IS from the preceding Dutch one, their use of lighting to heighten the story marks both of them as belonging to the seventeenth-century style known as the Baroque. The originator of this movement in art was an Italian painter named Caravaggio (plates 67, 95) whose short but electrifying career spanned the end of the sixteenth and the beginning of the seventeenth centuries. Rebelling against the conventional repetition of Renaissance artistic formulas, which had begun to be lifeless and stagnant by his day, he delighted in shocking the public by stripping his scenes of all vestiges of the old idealism, and populating even biblical scenes with characters drawn from the rough street life of Rome. Though his name no longer commands the universal recognition accorded to Michelangelo or Raphael, his influence on the artists of his own day was hardly less than theirs: Rembrandt in Holland, Murillo in Spain, and Rubens in Belgium (to name only the three best-known seventeenth-century painters whose works are illustrated here); all owed him an enormous debt, for he opened their eyes to a new world, and a new way of looking at it.

Feti, only a few years his junior, was no slavish imitator, yet we find his influence here too: though the mood of this picture is gentler and more poetic than Caravaggio would have allowed it to be, the pose of the sleeping Jacob, with his feet occupying the center foreground, the dramatic use of spotlighting, and such a detail as the mongrel who sleeps alongside him, are inspired by Caravaggio.

15.   REMBRANDT: *Jacob Wrestling with the Angel*

< PRECEDING PAGE

15. Jacob Wrestling with the Angel
BY RÉMBRANDT 1606–1669 *Dutch School*
State Museums, Berlin

But Jacob himself remained behind, all alone. Someone wrestled with him until the break of dawn. GENESIS 32:25

A STRIKING EXAMPLE of Rembrandt's ability to suggest more than meets the eye is this picture in which there are two struggles going on: one is the physical combat, made adequately clear by the angel's powerful hands and his knee locked around Jacob's side. The other is a battle of feelings; the expression on the angel's face is one of noble compassion devoid of the least taint of those base emotions that ordinarily accompany a fight. And Jacob, in spite of his muscular shoulders and swarthy beard, reminds us strangely of a fractious child; though he is still stiff with rebellion, something about the pose of the head makes us think it will soon be at rest in the angelic embrace.

16.   MURILLO: *Joseph Thrown into the Pit*

< PRECEDING PAGE

16. Joseph Thrown into the Pit

BY BARTOLOME ESTEBAN MURILLO 1618–1682

Spanish School, Wallace Collection, London

They seized him and threw him into the cistern, which was empty and dry. GENESIS 37:24

TODAY MURILLO IS BEST KNOWN for his pictures of the Virgin, but in his own time he was no less esteemed for his paintings of the street urchins and other low life that abounded in the streets of Seville. Like Caravaggio, he applied the knowledge of human nature that he had gained from firsthand observation to biblical subjects: in this very down-to-earth struggle, so different in every way from the one in the preceding painting, we see what looks like a street gang attacking a younger, more prosperous boy. His outright terror, as well as some shadows of doubt that cross the faces of the two who stand directly behind the chief tormentor, contribute to a masterful conception that holds true for all time and all places.

17.   UNKNOWN MASTER: *Jacob Receiving the Bloodstained Coat of Joseph*

< PRECEDING PAGE

17. Jacob Receiving the Bloodstained Coat of Joseph
BY UNKNOWN MASTER 17th century *Italian School*
Samuel H. Kress Collection, New York

*"It is my son's tunic. A wild beast has devoured him;
Joseph has been torn to pieces!"* GENESIS 37:33

ANOTHER DEVICE OFTEN USED by Baroque artists is the
kind of close-up with half-length figures that we see here.
Rarely, except in portraiture, do we find such half-figures
used before the seventeenth century. The *Crowning of
Thorns* (plate 80) by the fifteenth-century Dutch painter,
Hieronymus Bosch, is one of the earliest exceptions to the
rule; like this anonymous painter, he knew that faces and
hands, by themselves, are capable of expressing our emotions as well as the most violent action.

18.   REMBRANDT: *Jacob Blessing the Sons of Joseph*

< PRECEDING PAGE

18. Jacob Blessing the Sons of Joseph (detail)
BY REMBRANDT 1606–1669 *Dutch School*
Picture Gallery, Kassel

"The angel who has delivered me from all evil, bless the boys. . . ." When Joseph saw that his father had placed his right hand on Ephraim's head, he was displeased, so he took hold of his father's hand to remove it from Ephraim's head to that of Manasse. GENESIS 48:16–17

HERE WE FIND THE SAME compositional device used as in the preceding picture, both making use of the close-up with half-figures. Rembrandt's pictorial scheme, however, is much more subtle than that of the unknown Italian painter: he uses the bed as a logical excuse to obscure our view of the lower parts of the figures, and in so doing he makes the spectator feel as though he himself were standing at the foot of the bed, an unseen participant in the drama. In this scene of love and filial respect, it would be easy to overlook the little face of the dark-haired Manasse; yet once we have noticed it, the shadow of some discordant emotion is unmistakable. Prophetic of the Christian Dispensation, the younger brother, Ephraim, receives the first blessing, while the elder, like Cain and Esau and Joseph's older brothers, barely conceals his disappointment.

19. VERONESE: *Moses Saved from the Nile*

19. Moses Saved from the Nile

BY PAOLO VERONESE 1528–1588 *Italian School*

The Prado, Madrid

Pharao's daughter came down to the river to bathe. . . .
Noticing the basket among the reeds, she sent her hand-
maid to fetch it. On opening it, she looked, and lo, there
was a baby boy. EXODUS 2:5–6

TURNING BACK NOW TO THE LAST of the great painters of
the Venetian Renaissance, we are suddenly aware of a
profound kinship between our own soul-searching age and
the seventeenth-century art that we have just been exam-
ining. Veronese's lovely picture, by contrast, introduces
us to a luminous world inhabited by fairy-tale princesses
and their attendants. The costumes are those of contemporary Venetian ladies; the action so well-behaved that
we are made to think of a lighthearted charade. In the
hands of a gifted painter, we may be quite content with
the world of visual delights that we find here; at the same
time, it is possible to understand the impatience of the
young Caravaggio, who was just beginning his career at
the time of Veronese's death, when faced with an endless
series of such works by lesser artists.

20. DIERIC BOUTS: *Moses Before the Burning Bush*

< PRECEDING PAGE

20. Moses Before the Burning Bush

BY DIERIC BOUTS c.1415–1475 *Flemish School*

John G. Johnson Collection, Philadelphia

*There an angel of the Lord appeared to him in fire flaming
out of a bush. As he looked on, he was surprised to see that
the bush, though on fire, was not consumed.* EXODUS 3:2

IN OUR DISCUSSION of Bouts's *Abraham and Melchisedec*
(plate 8), we have already pointed out the looseness of
composition—its spread-out quality as compared with the
tightly knit groups of figures found in the paintings of the
Italian Renaissance. In this panel (and again in *Elias in
the Desert,* plate 40, by the same master) we find a
spreading-out in time, as well as space: within a single
frame the artist has shown us two episodes, both involving
the same personage, so that we see Moses taking off his
shoes in the middle ground, and the vision of the Burning
Bush occupying the front of the picture. Instead of choos-
ing the climax, our artist is more concerned with showing
us as much of the story as he can. It is almost as though
he did not assume any knowledge of the Bible on the
spectator's part, and consequently felt that he had to be as
explicit as the written word. Though this stress on storytelling in images was soon to yield, even in the Low Countries, to a less-detailed but more forcefully dramatic style,
it had deep roots and a long tradition in the art of the
Middle Ages, when most people did not have any books
and depended a great deal upon paintings and sculpture in
the churches for their knowledge of the Bible.

21. BERNARDINO LUINI: *The Slaying of the Firstborn*

< PRECEDING PAGE

21. The Slaying of the Firstborn
BY BERNARDINO LUINI 1480/85–1532 *Italian School*
Brera Gallery, Milan

Every first-born in this land shall die, from the first-born
of Pharao on the throne to the first-born of the slave-girl
at the handmill, as well as all the first-born of the animals.
EXODUS 11:5

IN ANOTHER EXAMPLE of this master's work (plate 6) we
saw him as a follower of Leonardo da Vinci. But Leonardo
was often occupied with other matters (he had been invited to the court of Milan as an expert military engineer,
and his artistic activities while there were almost inci-
dental), a follower often found himself without anything
to follow. Leonardo had never painted anything like the
fresco series of which this picture is but one panel, and
Luini was forced to turn to other sources for guidance.
Milan, which had enjoyed a brief period of importance
at the close of the fifteenth century, lapsed from this
position after it was invaded by the French and its terri-
tories broken up. Its school of painting, instead of keeping
up with the newer developments which were centered in
Rome, tended to remain faithful to the Florentine teach-
ings of an earlier day. It is hard to believe that this scene
was painted in the 1520s—almost two decades later than
Michelangelo's Sistine frescoes. Luini is still laboriously
working out problems of perspective, and is thrilled by the
novelty of using old Roman poses and costumes, much as
Florentine painters seventy years earlier had been.

22. DIERIC BOUTS: *The Passover Meal*

< PRECEDING PAGE

22. The Passover Meal
BY DIERIC BOUTS c.1415–1475 *Flemish School*
S. Pierre, Louvain, Belgium

*That same night they shall eat its roasted flesh with un-
leavened bread and bitter herbs.* EXODUS 12:8

HERE IS ANOTHER, and different example of Bouts's disregard for consistency (see discussion of *Moses Before the
Burning Bush,* plate 20), made understandable when we
realize that the Passover meal was also the Last Supper.
The curly leaves of endive scattered about the table are the
"bitter herbs," a traditional ingredient of the Jewish Passover; but the other ingredients have a Christian meaning
as well. The sacrificial lamb is a symbol of Christ; the
bread and wine refer to the Transubstantiation. Parallel-
ing this combination of Old and New Testament meanings
is the division of the group of figures: on the right (or
good) side are two women in new (that is, contemporary
Flemish) dress; in the equivalent positions on the left (the
Latin *sinister,* hence bad) side are two men in the traditional Jewish garb, as conceived by the Middle Ages. Between them stands a crowned man, probably King David,
the ancestor of Christ; while the bearded man between the
two women is the Prophet Elias (equated by Christ with
St. John; see discussion of the *Transfiguration* by Duccio,
plate 69), for whom a place is set at the Passover feast in
Jewish households to this very day.

23. BERNARDINO LUINI: *The Deliverance of the Israelites*

< PRECEDING PAGE

23. The Deliverance of the Israelites

BY BERNARDINO LUINI 1480/85–1532 *Italian School*

Brera Gallery, Milan

So Moses stretched out his hand over the sea, and at dawn the sea flowed back to its normal depth. The Egyptians were fleeing head on toward the sea, when the Lord hurled them into its midst. . . . Not a single one of them escaped.
EXODUS 14:27–28

HERE, THE DEFEAT of Pharao's army is a miracle indeed, for there is no hint of the turbulent sea that "covered the chariots and the charioteers of Pharao's whole army." The waters have simply covered the pursuing horde, while Moses raises his arm to point out the true source of the Israelites' deliverance.

24. DIERIC BOUTS: *The Gathering of the Manna*

< PRECEDING PAGE

24. The Gathering of the Manna
BY DIERIC BOUTS c.1415–1475 *Flemish School*
S. Pierre, Louvain, Belgium

*There on the surface of the desert were fine flakes like
hoarfrost on the ground. On seeing it, the Israelites asked
one another, "What is this?". . . . But Moses told them,
"This is the bread which the Lord has given you to eat."*
EXODUS 16:14–15

NEVER HAVING SEEN a real desert, Bouts knew only that it
must be very different from his flat, fertile homeland. He
imagined it as a semi-barren mountain landscape under a
wintry sky, and were it not for the addition of some fanci-
ful turbans, the Israelites would remind us of nothing so
much as a fifteenth-century family on a Sunday outing.

25. POUSSIN: *The Adoration of the Golden Calf*

< PRECEDING PAGE

25. The Adoration of the Golden Calf
BY NICOLAS POUSSIN 1594–1665 *French School*
National Gallery, London

Aaron . . . made a molten calf. . . . On seeing this, Aaron
built an altar before the calf and proclaimed, "Tomorrow
is a feast of the Lord. . . . Then they sat down to eat and
drink, and rose up to revel. EXODUS 32:3–6

WHILE THE PACE OF HISTORY itself was accelerating in the
sixteenth century, and European man's horizons were being immeasurably widened by the exploration of lands
hitherto only dreamed of, the understanding of past history, too, was being filled out. We have seen that Luini
(plate 21) was interested in Roman antiquity, as betrayed
by the classical costume of the gesticulating figure on the
left of his *Slaying of the Firstborn;* but the shepherds are
dressed in garments of the painter's own day. By the time
Poussin came to Italy a century later, it was possible to
project an entire pagan scene, such as this one, with con-
sistent accuracy in all its details. Poussin made the most
of his subject—the relapse of the Israelites into paganism
—by re-creating the world that we find represented on old
Roman reliefs. The older and more distant culture of ancient Egypt, which would have been historically more
correct for the scene, was barely known or understood
until the nineteenth century.

26. REMBRANDT: *Moses Showing the Tablets of the Law*

< PRECEDING PAGE

26. Moses Showing the Tablets of the Law
BY REMBRANDT 1606–1669 *Dutch School*
State Museums, Berlin

As Moses came down from Mount Sinai with the two tablets of the Commandments in his hands, he did not know that the skin of his face had become radiant while he conversed with the Lord. EXODUS 34:29

IN THE PRECEDING PAINTING we have to do some searching before we find the figure of Moses coming down from Mount Sinai at the left. In this one, we cannot find the Israelites. The face of Moses, so full of sorrow and bitter disappointment, is turned directly toward us, and remembering Rembrandt's trick of pulling the onlooker into his picture (plate 18), we are led to the realization that we are the Israelites. Actors addressing the audience are nothing new in the theater, but to achieve the same effect without sound or motion is an astonishing feat.

27.   POUSSIN: *The Messengers Returning from Chanaan with the Grapes*

< PRECEDING PAGE

27. The Messengers Returning from Chanaan with the
    Grapes

BY NICOLAS POUSSIN 1594–1665 *French School*

The Louvre, Paris

They also reached the Wadi Eschol, where they cut down
a branch with a single cluster of grapes on it, which two
of them carried on a pole. NUMBERS 13:23

WHILE POUSSIN was not primarily a landscape painter, he
fell in love with the countryside around Rome, and in a
series of four pictures, each with a different biblical subject, he sought to portray it under various seasonal aspects.
In this one, subtitled *Autumn,* the emphasis is appropri-
ately given to the land, flowing with milk and honey.
The figures are mere accessories, perfunctorily painted in.

28. REMBRANDT: *The Angel and the Prophet Balaam*

< PRECEDING PAGE

28. The Angel and the Prophet Balaam
BY REMBRANDT 1606–1669 *Dutch School*
Musée Cognacq-Jay, Paris

When the ass saw the angel of the Lord there, she cowered under Balaam. So, in anger, he again beat the ass with his stick. But now the Lord opened the mouth of the ass, and she asked Balaam, "What have I done to you that you should beat me these three times?" NUMBERS 22:27–28

THOUGH TODAY it is the subtle, understated drama of Rembrandt's late works that fascinates us most, the fame which he enjoyed in Holland during his own lifetime was in recognition of such pictures as this one. In this early style we are able to find many close links with the Italian Early Baroque: the intense warm colors; the odd-angle perspective; the theatrical display of gesture and facial expression.

29. JEAN FOUQUET: *The Fall of Jericho*

< PRECEDING PAGE

29. The Fall of Jericho

BY JEAN FOUQUET c.1420–1481 *French School*

Bibliothèque Nationale, Paris

As the horns blew, the people began to shout. When they heard the signal horn, they raised a tremendous shout. The wall collapsed, and the people stormed the city in a frontal attack and took it. JOSUE 6:20

THIS MINIATURE PAINTING, one of a set of book illustrations, was painted in France at about the same time that Dieric Bouts was painting his huge altarpiece for S. Pierre in nearby Belgium. It is obvious that Fouquet borrowed his landscape style from the Netherlandish school (the airy vista with its green knolls punctuated by tiny roofs and steeples is not unlike the landscape in Bouts's *Moses Before the Burning Bush,* plate 20); yet, for all the painstaking details, we might be inclined to believe that the original of this picture is larger than the panels of the Louvain altar! When we go about analyzing it, we find that it has a monumentality which consists of many separate things: the ability to organize a scene so that the figures and their setting form a close-knit group; giving an appearance of real solidity to the human figures; giving the impression that they are firmly set upon the ground. Fouquet must have learned these things from Italian painting. Partaking, like France itself, of both the north and the south of Europe, Fouquet successfully blended the best features of both their styles.

< PRECEDING PAGE

30. Manoe's Sacrifice

BY REMBRANDT 1606–1669 *Dutch School*

Picture Gallery, Dresden

As the flame rose to the sky from the altar, the angel of the Lord ascended in the flame of the altar. JUDGES 13:20

NOT QUITE SO ITALIAN in its manner as his picture of Balaam (plate 28), this painting nevertheless belongs to Rembrandt's storytelling phase. Manoe acts out his piety and humility, but his wife already has something of that deceptively simple air of inner repose that makes us return again and again to such a figure as Joseph's wife in *Jacob Blessing the Sons of Joseph* (plate 18), without ever being fully satisfied that we have understood her completely.

31. RUBENS: *Samson Wrestling with the Lion*

< PRECEDING PAGE

31. Samson Wrestling with the Lion
BY PETER PAUL RUBENS 1577–1640 *Flemish School*
National Museum, Stockholm

A young lion came roaring to meet him. But the spirit of the Lord came upon Samson, and although he had no weapons, he tore the lion in pieces as one tears a kid.
JUDGES 14:5–6

THE NAME OF RUBENS came to epitomize the Baroque style of the seventeenth century, as opposed to the Classical style of Poussin. Indeed, in the following years, artistic battles raged between the "Rubenists" and the "Poussinists" in France. Despite his sweeping swirls of motion, visible in even a small oil sketch like this one, Rubens was as much interested in the study of antiquity as the cool, deliberate Poussin. This *Samson* was probably patterned after a Roman Hercules, the ancient pagan hero who had an encounter with a lion similar to Samson's.

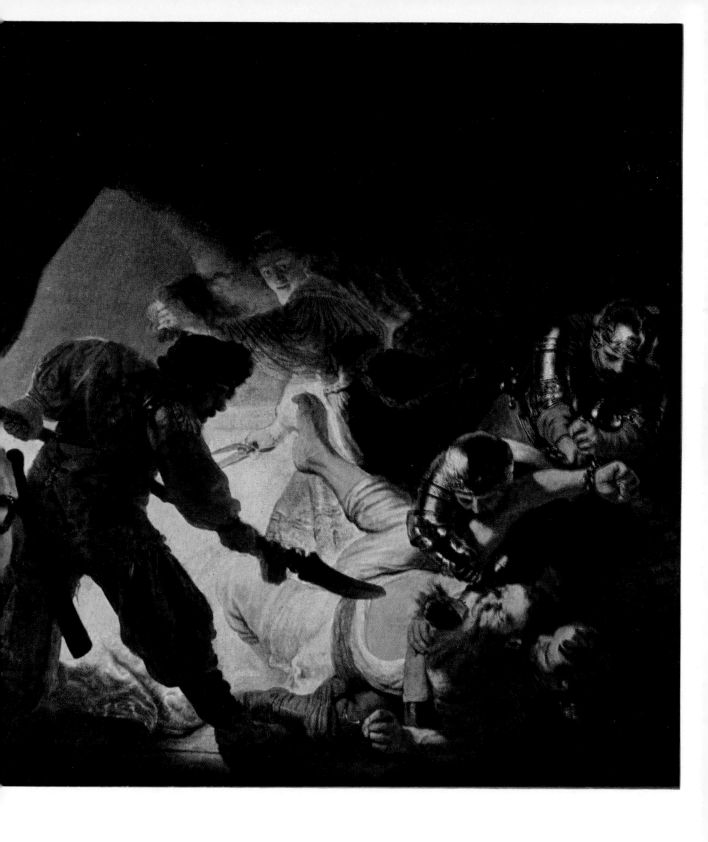

32.   REMBRANDT: *The Blinding of Samson*

< PRECEDING PAGE

32. The Blinding of Samson (detail)
BY REMBRANDT 1606–1669 *Dutch School*
Staedel Institute, Frankfurt

But the Philistines seized him and gouged out his eyes.
JUDGES 16:21

WHEN HE CHOSE TO, Rembrandt could compose a picture
as dynamic, and as full of complex interwoven movements
as Rubens. His *Blinding of Samson* combines the greatest
virtuosity of composition and lighting with a complicated
interplay of physical and emotional stresses. Bodily tor-
ture at its rawest is combined here with a gamut of delicately shaded feelings, from the horrified fascination of the
halberdier on the left, poised uncertainly between thrust
and recoil, to the half-triumphant, half-frightened Dalila
who turns in her flight to see the results of her treachery.

33. POUSSIN: *Ruth and Booz*

< PRECEDING PAGE

33. Ruth and Booz

BY NICOLAS POUSSIN 1594–1665 *French School*

The Louvre, Paris

Booz said to Ruth, "Listen, my daughter! Do not go to glean in anyone else's field; you are not to leave here. Stay here with my women servants." RUTH 2:8

THIS IS THE *Summer* of the Four Seasons cycle that was referred to in the discussion of Poussin's *Messengers Returning from Chanaan with the Grapes* (plate 27). In this painting Poussin has achieved a more harmonious integration of figures and landscape; though nature still takes first place, the episode in the foreground is prettily set off by the wall of grain behind, as though it were being played on an outdoor stage.

34. REMBRANDT: *Anna and Samuel*

$<$ PRECEDING PAGE

34. Anna and Samuel

BY REMBRANDT 1606–1669 *Dutch School*

Collection Earl of Ellesmere, London

And the Lord visited Anna, and she conceived . . . and the child Samuel became great before the Lord. I KINGS 2:21

REMBRANDT has left us several portraits of his family, and from these we know that he made his small son, Titus, the model for the child in this picture. We are not left to wonder, in this case, how Rembrandt achieved his magic sense of intimacy: he had actually observed how the mere inclination of two heads, or the silence of a rapt gaze can convey a feeling of closeness and mutual understanding as effectively as the most demonstrative act.

35. ANDREA DEL CASTAGNO: *The Youthful David*

< PRECEDING PAGE

35. The Youthful David

BY ANDREA DEL CASTAGNO c. 1423–1457

Italian School, National Gallery, Washington, D.C.
(Widener Collection)

And he put his hand into his scrip, and took a stone, and cast it with the sling, and fetching it about struck the Philistine in the forehead. And the stone was fixed in his forehead. . . . and took his sword, and drew it out of the sheath, and slew him. I KINGS 17:49, 51

ONE OF THE GENERATION of Florentine painters who followed in the footsteps of Masaccio (plate 70), Castagno's aim was toward greater anatomical accuracy and more variety of bodily movement in his figures. The victorious David—one of the favorite symbols of the young Florentine republic, which liked to think of itself as a "giant killer" too—shows such verve and skillful observations of detail that it comes as something of a surprise to find that the pose was borrowed from an ancient Roman statue.

The odd shape of the picture is due to the fact that it was painted as a processional shield; parades of every sort are still a popular public spectacle in Italy, and in the fifteenth century they were decked out with costumes and floats designed, often, by the most famous artists of the day.

36. REMBRANDT: *David Playing the Harp Before Saul*

< PRECEDING PAGE

36. David Playing the Harp Before Saul

BY REMBRANDT 1606–1669 *Dutch School*

Mauritshuis, The Hague

And the evil spirit from the Lord came upon Saul, and he sat in his house, and held a spear in his hand: and David played. I KINGS 19:9

THIS UNFORGETTABLE PICTURE, painted late in Rembrandt's life, gives us an insight into the story behind the story such as only an old man, full of his own remembrances of a happier youth, could convey. The terse account in the Bible tells us only that King Saul, jealous of the acclaim that David received, hurled his spear at the young hero while he was playing the harp. Instead of making the kind of action-picture to which the climax of the story would lend itself, Rembrandt has chosen an indeterminate moment before the violent outburst. Who can say what sorrows the music has released in the breast of the old King? Does he mourn his lost youth, or is he struggling with his own jealous passion? His right hand loosely holds the murderous spear, and he seems as unaware of any intention to hurl it as the younger man, completely absorbed in his playing.

37 · SALVATOR ROSA: *Saul and the Witch of Endor*

< PRECEDING PAGE

37. Saul and the Witch of Endor

BY SALVATOR ROSA 1615–1675 *Italian School*

The Louvre, Paris

An old man cometh up, and he is covered with a mantle. And Saul understood that it was Samuel, and he bowed himself with his face to the ground, and adored. I KINGS 28:14

ROSA WHO, in addition to painting, also composed poetry and music, gives an imaginative turn to the Baroque style very different from the stubborn realism of Caravaggio (plates 67, 95). Here he delights in heightening the weird atmosphere by including phantoms and magicians' paraphernalia of which the Bible makes no mention.

38.   RUBENS: *The Judgment of Solomon*

< PRECEDING PAGE

38. The Judgment of Solomon
BY PETER PAUL RUBENS 1577–1640 *Flemish School*
Royal Museum of Fine Arts, Copenhagen

*Divide, said he, the living child in two, and give half to the
one, and half to the other.* III KINGS 3:25

LOOKING AT THIS PICTURE, after a series of other Baroque
works, we are struck with Rubens' likeness to the Venetian
masters of the High Renaissance. Not for him the sensitive
soul-searching of a Rembrandt, nor the drama of daily
existence that we find in Murillo. An extraordinarily vital
and versatile man, who combined his well-paid artistic
career with an equally successful one as a diplomat, Rubens was attracted by the glowing richness of pictures such
as Veronese's *Moses Saved from the Nile* (plate 19), to
which he added his own lusty love of action.

PIERO DELLA FRANCESCA: *Solomon and the Queen of Saba*

< PRECEDING PAGE

39. Solomon and the Queen of Saba (detail)
BY PIERO DELLA FRANCESCA 1415/20–1492
Italian School, S. Francesco, Arezzo

And the queen of Saba, having heard of the fame of Solomon in the name of the Lord, came to try him with hard questions. III KINGS 10:1

THE PAINTERS of the Early Renaissance in Italy, like their Flemish contemporaries (such as Dieric Bouts), were pioneer discoverers of the world around them, but with one fundamental difference: their primary concern was the rational conquest of space by means of perspective, not the observation of nature in realistic detail. In order to accomplish this, they had to "construct" their pictures according to a strict system of mathematical rules, which made them concentrate on the underlying geometry of natural shapes, rather than on their surface appearance. Piero della Francesca was a consummate master of this new approach; in his picture he has created a world of forms unrivaled for its crystalline harmony and strength.

40.   DIERIC BOUTS: *Elias in the Desert*

< PRECEDING PAGE

40. Elias in the Desert
BY DIERIC BOUTS c.1415–1475 *Flemish School*
S. Pierre, Louvain, Belgium

*And he cast himself down, and slept in the shadow of the
juniper tree and behold an angel of the Lord touched him,
and said to him: Arise and eat.* III KINGS 19:5

LACKING THOUGH IT MAY BE in the kind of rational con-
struction that we have just discussed in connection with
Piero della Francesca's work (plate 39), Bouts's picture
possesses one outstanding quality, in addition to those
already enumerated: the figure of the angel, so expressive
of tenderness, contains a depth of feeling in combination
with restraint of gesture that reminds us of a later Dutch
painter: Rembrandt.

41.   RUBENS: *The Ascension of Elias*

< PRECEDING PAGE

41. The Ascension of Elias
BY PETER PAUL RUBENS 1577–1640 *Flemish School*
Private Collection

Behold a fiery chariot and fiery horses parted them both asunder: and Elias went up by a whirlwind into heaven.
IV KINGS 2:11

THIS SMALL CANVAS is so filled with thunderous motion that it almost seems as though it would burst its frame. Only a sketch for a larger painting, the grand sweep of its composition could comfortably fill a whole wall. The extraordinary freedom of Rubens' brushwork is at its freshest here, as is his spontaneous vigor; and indeed, both skill and conviction are needed to persuade us that a horse and chariot as solid as these could be skyward bound.

42. RUBENS: *The Defeat of Sennacherib*

< PRECEDING PAGE

42. The Defeat of Sennacherib
BY PETER PAUL RUBENS 1577–1640 *Flemish School*
Pinakothek, Munich

And it came to pass that night, that an angel of the Lord came, and slew in the camp of the Assyrians a hundred and eighty-five thousand. And when he arose early in the morning, he saw all the bodies of the dead. IV KINGS 19:35

IN A GRAND MELEE of the earthly and the supernatural; of the contemporary with old Roman and Oriental costumes; of figures inspired by ancient statuary, and others by Renaissance painting, Rubens has created this scene of incredible complexity and excitement. It is one of the great achievements of his particular genius that he was able to summon up such a vast and varied population for his pictures, and moreover to maintain such order in his seething mass of shapes that we are able to read the events at the same time that we are swept along in the action.

43. BOTTICELLI: *Mardochai Lamenting Before the Gates of the Palace*

< PRECEDING PAGE

43. Mardochai Lamenting Before the Gates of
    the Palace

BY SANDRO BOTTICELLI C.1445–1510 *Italian School*

Collection Pallavicini, Rome

*Mardochai . . . rent his garments, and put on sackcloth,
strewing ashes on his head. And he cried with a loud voice
in the street in the midst of the city, showing the anguish
of his mind. And he came lamenting in this manner even
to the gate of the palace.* ESTHER 4:1–2

THOUGH BOTTICELLI'S main concern here is that rational
conquest of space that was mentioned in the discussion of
Piero della Francesca (plate 39), the solitary figure of
Mardochai gains a certain pathos from its stony setting,
as empty as the doom that awaits his people.

44. JAN STEEN: *The Wrath of Assuerus*

< PRECEDING PAGE

44. The Wrath of Assuerus

BY JAN STEEN 1626–1679 *Dutch School*

Barber Institute of Fine Arts, Birmingham, England

And Esther said: It is this Aman that is our adversary and most wicked enemy. Aman hearing this was forthwith astonished, not being able to bear the countenance of the king and of the queen. But the king being angry rose up, and went from the place of the banquet into the garden set with trees. ESTHER 7:6–7

AN INNKEEPER BY TRADE, Steen is more noted for his lively pictures of Dutch family life than for his painting of religious subjects. Here, with amusing results, he has merged the two: Assuerus is none other than the heavy Dutch father (dressed up in a homemade turban, and what looks like the parlor drapes), thundering at his errant son (Aman), while the servants whisper in the corridor, and the mother (Esther) looks pleased and relieved that the job of disciplining the children has been taken out of her hands. Like Van den Eeckhout (plate 13), Steen cannot refrain from including the kind of elaborately laden table that was so dear to the Dutch burghers; we may gather, however, that roast peacock was not a staple on the menu of those times: its appearance, rather than the falling platter, seems to have frightened the little dog, who adds to the family turmoil by barking.

HIEREMIAS

45. MICHELANGELO: *Jeremias*

< PRECEDING PAGE

45. Jeremias

BY MICHELANGELO 1475–1564 *Italian School*

Sistine Chapel, Vatican, Rome

To whom shall I speak? And to whom shall I testify, that he may hear? JEREMIAS 6:10

THE FORCEFULNESS which, in Michelangelo's two figures of God (plates 1 and 2) is directed outward, seems here to be concentrated deep within the form of this brooding giant. What is he brooding about? We cannot say with any greater certainty than we were able to analyze the sorrow of Rembrandt's aged Saul (plate 36): both are overwhelmed by a sadness which is more than momentary, but whereas we can identify King Saul's mood with the welling-up of emotion that all of us experience from time to time, Michelangelo's prophet seems to carry the burdens of all mankind, forever.

46. RAPHAEL: *The Vision of Ezechiel*

< PRECEDING PAGE

46. The Vision of Ezechiel

BY RAPHAEL 1483–1520 *Italian School*

Pitti Palace, Florence

And I saw, and behold a whirlwind came out of the north, and a great cloud, and a fire infolding it, and brightness was about it. . . . And in the midst thereof the likeness of four living creatures. . . . there was the face of a man, and the face of a lion . . . the face of an ox . . . and the face of an eagle over all the four. EZECHIEL 1:4–5, 10

CLEARLY, RAPHAEL was trying to imitate Michelangelo's style in this picture; but his was not the same temperament. Though we may recognize the face of God, and the knot of heavenly beings all swirling through the air together as being derived from Michelangelo's Sistine ceiling (plates 1 and 2), the dynamic forward rush is missing here. Raphael's works breathe a gentler, more harmonious beauty; the fierce nobility of Michelangelo's angels has been transformed here into smiling sweetness, and even the strange creatures—symbols of the four evangelists whom they prophesy—have a docile, domesticated air.

47. REMBRANDT: *Baltassar's Feast*

< PRECEDING PAGE

47. Baltassar's Feast

BY REMBRANDT 1606–1669 *Dutch School*

By permission of the Earl of Derby, Knowsley,
    Prescot, Lancashire

In the same hour there appeared fingers, as it were of the
hand of a man, writing over against the candlestick upon
the surface of the wall of the king's palace; and the king
beheld the joints of the hand that wrote. DANIEL 5:5

THIS PICTURE in Rembrandt's early, Baroque style cannot
help but remind us of the picture by Jan Steen (plate 44).
Whereas the latter, however, is unable to convince us of
the serious importance of the event, Rembrandt succeeds
in catching us up in his drama by using the same device
that we have already found in his *Jacob Blessing the Sons*
of Joseph (plate 18): we seem to be sitting at the end of
the table, and like the other guests, we are hypnotized by
the sight of the ghostly hand writing its message of doom
on the wall.

48.   TENIERS THE ELDER: *Daniel in the Lions' Den*

< PRECEDING PAGE

48. Daniel in the Lions' Den (detail)
BY DAVID TENIERS THE ELDER 1582–1649
Flemish School, Bavarian State Picture Collections,
  Munich

*My God hath sent his angel, and hath shut up the mouths
of the lions, and they have not hurt me, forasmuch as before him justice hath been found in me. Yea and before
thee, O king, I have done no offense.* DANIEL 6:22

TO A SEVENTEENTH-CENTURY ARTIST, this miracle—the
best-known event of Daniel's career—posed a problem almost impossible to solve: how to show a group of lions
being both ferocious and peaceable at the same time. The
oddly human expressions of the animals in our picture
bespeak Teniers' effort to convey to us that these lions are
aware of the unusual role they have been forced to play,
and if they seem ill at ease we can hardly blame them for
their pose of studied indifference. A Medieval painter,
viewing the story on a more abstract and symbolic plane,
would have experienced none of the difficulties that Teniers has struggled with so bravely and unsuccessfully.

49. REMBRANDT: *The Vision of Daniel*

< PRECEDING PAGE

49. The Vision of Daniel

BY REMBRANDT 1606–1669 *Dutch School*

State Museums, Berlin

And when he spoke to me I fell flat on the ground, and he touched me, and set me upright, and he said to me: I will show thee what things are to come to pass in the end of the malediction, for the time hath its end. DANIEL 8:18–19

PAINTED SOME FIFTEEN YEARS after *Baltassar's Feast* (plate 47), this picture shows the profound change Rembrandt's art had undergone in the interval. Instead of emphasizing the spectacular, frightening character of Daniel's experience, the artist barely hints at the vision itself (the dimly lit ram on the extreme right). His main interest centers on the relationship of Daniel and the angel. They are both extraordinarily gentle figures; and the angel, we feel, has come first of all to comfort and reassure the trembling prophet, rather than to interpret the vision. It is the bond of human sympathy between the two that makes the painting memorable even for those beholders unfamiliar with the character or meaning of what Daniel saw.

50. RUBENS?: *Jonas Cast into the Sea*

< PRECEDING PAGE

50. Jonas Cast into the Sea

BY RUBENS? 1577–1640 *Flemish School*

Museum, Nancy

*And they took Jonas, and cast him into the sea, and the
sea ceased from raging.* JONAS 1:15

THERE IS A STRONG stylistic similarity between this picture
and Rembrandt's *Christ in the Storm on the Sea of Galilee* (plate 66); indeed, the angle of the two boats, the men
tugging at the sail, and even a small detail such as the
broken rigging, are so similar that we may not be wrong
if we suspect that one was inspired by the other, or that
both artists had received their inspiration from a third
picture, unknown to us today. The similarities point out
the importance of each artist's individual interpretation:
in Rembrandt's painting, we are mainly aware of the piti-
ful plight of the little boat, overwhelmed by the forces of
nature; in the Rubens canvas, nature merely serves to
accentuate the angry mood of the sailors who pitch Jonas
into the maw of a dragon-like sea monster.

51. RAPHAEL: *The Marriage of the Virgin*

< PRECEDING PAGE

51. The Marriage of the Virgin
BY RAPHAEL 1483–1520 *Italian School*
Brera Gallery, Milan

A virgin betrothed to a man named Joseph, of the house of David, and the virgin's name was Mary. LUKE 1:27

THIS ENCHANTINGLY GRACEFUL and gentle picture, which bears the date 1504, makes an interesting contrast with the *Vision of Ezechiel* (plate 46), painted more than a dozen years later toward the end of Raphael's brief career. The symmetrical design, the clear, quiet air, the delicate, slender figures still bear the stamp of an older artist, Pietro Perugino, under whose guidance the young Raphael had grown to maturity—a maturity fully evident in the marvelous harmony of figures and space to which our painting owes its fame. The *Vision of Ezechiel* is infinitely more forceful and eloquent; yet there, too, however striking the differences, we sense the same genius for harmony.

52. VAN DER WEYDEN: *The Annunciation*

52. The Annunciation (detail)

BY ROGIER VAN DER WEYDEN 1399/1400–1464

Flemish School, The Louvre, Paris

And when the angel had come to her, he said, "Hail, full of grace, the Lord is with thee. Blessed art thou among women." LUKE 1:28

THE GREAT FLEMISH MASTER who painted this panel was one of the pioneers of a new realistic style in Late Medieval art. His profound influence on fifteenth-century painting north of the Alps may be seen in the work of such artists as Dieric Bouts, Hans Memling, Geertgen tot Sint Jans, and Hieronymus Bosch (plates 40, 57, 72, 80). But Rogier's realism with its magnificently close observation of every detail from the pattern of the tiled floor to the distant hills visible through the window, nevertheless retains a deeply devotional character: the everyday objects in our picture—the vase of lilies, the chandelier with its solitary candle, the brass ewer and basin—are at the same time symbolic tributes to the purity of the Virgin.

53. ALBERTINELLI: *The Visitation*

< PRECEDING PAGE

53. The Visitation

BY MARIOTTO ALBERTINELLI 1474–1515

Italian School, Uffizi Gallery, Florence

And Elizabeth was filled with the Holy Spirit, and cried out with a loud voice, saying, "Blessed art thou among women and blessed is the fruit of thy womb! And how have I deserved that the mother of my Lord should come to me?"
LUKE 1:41–43

IN PERIODS of great artistic achievement, even artists of the second rank will sometimes produce a masterpiece. This *Visitation,* painted in 1503, is such a work. Albertinelli, a Florentine contemporary of Leonardo da Vinci and Michelangelo, never again reached the same high level of inspiration. His two women combine statuesque dignity and strength with a tenderness of feeling worthy of Raphael. The open sky, framed by the arcade against which the figures are silhouetted, acts as a huge halo encircling both heads and thus emphasizes the solemn character of the meeting.

54. PIERO DELLA FRANCESCA: *The Nativity*

< PRECEDING PAGE

54. The Nativity

BY PIERO DELLA FRANCESCA 1415/20–1492

Italian School, National Gallery, London

And it came to pass while they were there, that the days for her to be delivered were fulfilled. And she brought forth her firstborn son, and wrapped him in swaddling clothes, and laid him in a manger, because there was no room for them in the inn. LUKE 2:6–7

THIS PANEL, probably painted a dozen years or more after the same artist's magnificent frescoes in Arezzo (see *Solomon and the Queen of Saba,* plate 39), shows a similar clarity of structure but a more delicate, poetic air. The humble circumstances of Christ's birth—the stable, the ox, and ass—have been pushed back into the middle ground; this is the simple, earth-bound world of the shepherds who have come in from their fields, and of Joseph as well. The adoring Virgin and the Child, in contrast, partake of the celestial world of the angel musicians, so that both aspects of the Nativity, the natural and the supernatural, appear distinct yet harmoniously related to each other.

55. EL GRECO: *The Adoration of the Shepherds*

< PRECEDING PAGE

55. The Adoration of the Shepherds
BY EL GRECO 1541–1614 *Spanish School*
The Metropolitan Museum of Art, New York

So they went with haste, and they found Mary and Joseph,
and the babe lying in the manger. LUKE 2:16

WHILE THE SUBJECT of this picture is essentially the same
as that of Piero's *Nativity,* it would be difficult to imagine
a greater contrast of mood. The crisp daylight of Piero
has been changed into night, a night lit up by dancing,
flamelike tongues of supernatural radiance. Angels, shepherds, and the Holy Family itself are united by a common
ecstasy of feeling, swept away, as it were, by the tremendous miracle of which they are the witnesses. Their forms,
strangely translucent, have lost all material solidity, so
that the figures seem to float and soar in mystic rapture.
Which artist has done greater justice to his exalted theme?
We would be hard put to make a choice, for either work
in its own way is a supreme achievement.

56. GENTILE DA FABRIANO: *The Adoration of the Magi*

< PRECEDING PAGE

56. The Adoration of the Magi

BY GENTILE DA FABRIANO C.1370–1427

Italian School, Uffizi Gallery, Florence

And entering the house, they found the child with Mary his mother, and falling down they worshipped him. And opening their treasures they offered him gifts of gold, frankincense and myrrh. MATTHEW 2:11

DURING THE MIDDLE AGES, the three Magi (wise men from the East) who followed the star to Bethlehem came to be regarded as kings, and their adoration of the Infant Christ was often represented as a splendid pageant. The ornate, graceful style of Gothic painting around the year 1400 lent itself especially well to this subject; our altar is the largest and most colorful of its kind, brimming with extravagant Oriental costumes and finely observed animals (note the monkeys, camels, and hunting leopards). In the background we see the three Magi again, on the road to Bethlehem, accompanied by an endless train of mounted soldiers and retainers. Let us not forget the serious purpose behind all this, however: the Epiphany is the first manifestation of Christ to the gentiles, and our artist, in putting on this lavish display, wants to show us how all the mighty of this earth pay homage to the newborn king.

57. MEMLING: *The Presentation of the Christ Child in the Temple*

< PRECEDING PAGE

57. The Presentation of the Christ Child in the Temple
BY HANS MEMLING c.1433–1494 *Flemish School*
The Prado, Madrid

*He also received him into his arms and blessed God, say-
ing, "Now thou dost dismiss thy servant, O Lord, according to thy word, in peace; because my eyes have seen thy
salvation, which thou hast prepared before the face of all
peoples."* LUKE 2:28–31

THE QUIET SOLEMNITY of this panel, by a talented follower of Rogier van der Weyden (plate 52), conveys the
importance of the ritual here depicted: in obedience to
Mosaic law, the Infant Jesus, as a male firstborn child, is
presented to the Lord. Joseph, on the left, carries a small
cage with the prescribed offering, two doves. On either
side of the altar we see the just and devout Simeon and the
old prophetess Anna, who recognize the Infant as the
Redeemer. But who is the young man viewing the sacred
event from between two columns on the extreme right?
This reverent spectator is clearly a portrait, and from his
modest bearing and half-hidden position we gather that it
must be Hans Memling himself, who in this discreet way
asserts both his piety and his artistic pride as the creator
of the panel.

58.   GIOTTO: *The Flight into Egypt*

< PRECEDING PAGE

58. The Flight into Egypt

BY GIOTTO 1266?–1337 *Italian School*

Arena Chapel, Padua

So he arose, and took the child and his mother by night, and withdrew into Egypt. MATTHEW 2:14

GIOTTO, who lived a hundred years before the Early Renaissance of the fifteenth century, was the first Medieval painter to achieve great personal fame among his contemporaries, who praised him as the equal of the legendary artists of Classical antiquity. It was he, they said, who led painting back to nature and thus laid the foundation for the flowering of Italian art in the years to come. The essential truth of this claim is still acknowledged by modern historians; indeed, the directness and simplicity of Giotto's work speak to us as strongly today as they did to the men of his own time. Our picture is taken from his most monumental achievement, the Paduan frescoes depicting the Life of Christ. Three other scenes from the same cycle appear in plates 73, 77, and 86.

59.   POUSSIN: *The Massacre of the Innocents*

< PRECEDING PAGE

59. The Massacre of the Innocents
BY NICOLAS POUSSIN 1594–1665 *French School*
Musée Condé, Chantilly

*Then Herod . . . sent and slew all the boys in Bethlehem
and all its neighborhood who were two years old or under.*
MATTHEW 2:16

AT FIRST GLANCE it may seem hard to believe that this
picture, so thoroughly Italian in spirit, was painted by a
Frenchman. The Classical architecture of the setting and
the statuesque, powerful figures make us think of Raphael
and Michelangelo; only the lighting, with its sharp contrasts, and the artist's strong sense of drama tell us that
this must be a product of the Baroque era rather than of
the High Renaissance. Yet the *Massacre* is perhaps a bit
too self-consciously "Roman" to be the work of an Italian
master (who, after all, would not need to parade his knowledge of the great Italian tradition before us as Poussin
does here). In order to do justice to the picture, we must
realize that it was done soon after Poussin's arrival in the
Eternal City, and that, for a provincial young painter from
the North, it represents a truly astonishing, disciplined
effort to "do as the Romans do."

60. GEORGES DE LA TOUR: *Joseph the Carpenter*

< PRECEDING PAGE

60. Joseph the Carpenter

BY GEORGES DE LA TOUR 1593–1652 *French School*

The Louvre, Paris

Jesus began to teach them in their synagogues, so that they were astonished, and said, "How did this man come by this wisdom and these miracles? Is not this the carpenter's son?" MATTHEW 13:54–55

SO FAR AS WE KNOW, Georges de La Tour never visited Italy. Although an exact contemporary of Poussin, with a similar provincial background, he did not feel the urge to turn himself into a "Roman by choice" but was content to spend his life in the small town of Nancy. His fame as one of the great painters of his century is of fairly recent date. Most of Georges de La Tour's pictures are nighttime scenes such as this one, lit by a single candle and depicting some quiet, domestic activity. To the casual beholder, they may look like everyday events. Only their poetic mood, their reverential feeling for the dignity of simple people doing simple things, betrays their religious inspiration.

61.   LUCA GIORDANO: *The Twelve-Year-Old Christ Among the Doctors*

< PRECEDING PAGE

61. The Twelve-Year-Old Christ Among the Doctors
BY LUCA GIORDANO   1632–1705 *Italian School*
National Gallery, Rome

And it came to pass after three days, that they found him in the temple, sitting in the midst of the teachers, listening to them and asking them questions. And all who were listening to him were amazed at his understanding and his answers. LUKE 2:46–47

IF GEORGES DE LA TOUR has a greater stature now than he did during his own lifetime, Luca Giordano's reputation has decreased steadily. His name, once famous throughout Europe, is well known today only among specialists in Italian Baroque art. Even though he lacks the profound human insight or the magic light of a Rembrandt, Luca hardly deserves such complete neglect; at his best, as in our picture, he displays extraordinary dramatic power and inventiveness. His was a truly theatrical imagination (in the best meaning of the term) that enabled him to stage any subject sumptuously and effectively. While we may miss a certain depth of character in his canvases, we must admire their sweeping movement, their vibrant sense of life.

62. VERROCCHIO: *The Baptism of Christ*

< PRECEDING PAGE

62. The Baptism of Christ
BY VERROCCHIO c.1435–1488 *Italian School*
Uffizi Gallery, Florence

And when Jesus had been baptized, he immediately came up from the water. And behold, the heavens were opened to him, and he saw the Spirit of God descending as a dove and coming upon him. MATTHEW 3:16

VERROCCHIO, THE TEACHER of Leonardo da Vinci, is far better known as a sculptor than as a painter. The two main figures of our picture, with their rather harsh modeling and overly explicit anatomical detail, do indeed give the impression of statues projected onto a surface; and the rocks behind St. John, as well as the oddly metallic-looking palm tree on the left, suggest a similar interest in their tangible rather than their purely visual aspects. There are, however, two areas that attract attention because of their very different treatment: the delicately atmospheric landscape in the far background, and the angel holding Christ's robe, who seems to be of a breed far removed from that of his rather prosaic companion. These parts, scholars believe, were done by the young Leonardo, then still a member of Verrocchio's shop but already a painter of genius.

63.   DUCCIO: *The Temptation of Christ*

< PRECEDING PAGE

63. The Temptation of Christ
BY DUCCIO c.1255–1319 *Italian School*
The Frick Collection, New York

*Then Jesus said to him, "Begone, Satan! for it is written,
'The Lord thy God shalt thou worship and him only shalt
thou serve.' "* MATTHEW 4:10

SLIGHTLY OLDER THAN GIOTTO and, like him, a Tuscan,
Duccio was an artist of more conservative temper: not a
revolutionary but a reformer, who instilled new life into
the traditional painting style. That style had been developed during the first five centuries of the Christian era and
was perpetuated for another thousand years by the painters
of the East Roman (or Byzantine) Empire, who served the
Greek Orthodox Church. In Duccio's hands, the Byzantine
figures achieved greater roundness and a more human expression, and the landscape settings became less abstract
(even though the cities on our picture, representing earthly
power and wealth, still look like simplified, small-scale
models). The *Temptation,* as well as the other panels by
Duccio here reproduced (plates 65 and 69), once were part
of the artist's masterpiece, the great altar for the Cathedral
at Siena.

64. GERARD DAVID: *The Marriage at Cana*

< PRECEDING PAGE

64. The Marriage at Cana (detail)
BY GERARD DAVID 1450/60–1523 *Flemish School*
The Louvre, Paris

*Jesus said to them, "Fill the jars with water." And they
filled them to the brim. And Jesus said to them, "Draw out
now, and take to the chief steward." And they took it to
him. . . . the water after it had become wine.* JOHN 2:7–9

WITH GERARD DAVID, Memling's successor as the most
esteemed painter of the town of Bruges, we witness the
first impact of the Italian Renaissance on Flemish art,
which until then had been nourished mainly by the tradition of Rogier van der Weyden. The figures seem broader,
heavier, more emphatically modeled than before; they also
loom larger in the design of the panel. At the same time,
we note a lessened concern with the devotional aspects of
the scene: among the richly dressed wedding guests, few
seem aware of the miracle of water changed into wine that
is happening in their midst.

65.   DUCCIO: *The Calling of the Apostles Peter and Andrew*

< PRECEDING PAGE

65. The Calling of the Apostles Peter and Andrew
BY DUCCIO C.1255–1319 *Italian School*
National Gallery of Art, Washington, D.C.
  (Samuel H. Kress Collection)

*As he was walking by the sea of Galilee, he saw two
brothers, Simon, who is called Peter, and his brother
Andrew, casting a net into the sea (for they were fisher-
men). And he said to them, "Come, follow me, and I will
make you fishers of men."* MATTHEW 4:18–19

ACCORDING TO THE ACCOUNT in Matthew and Mark, this
event took place very soon after the Temptation. It is of
particular significance, since Peter and Andrew were the
first of the twelve Apostles to receive Christ's call. As they
labor at pulling in their net, Christ beckons to them from
the shore, promising to make them fishers of men. Here,
as in the *Temptation* (plate 63), we see a luminous gold
background in place of the natural color of the sky, and a
landscape of oddly stylized, jagged rocks. These are traditional Byzantine practices continued by Duccio. The water
with its teeming marine life, on the other hand, seems sur-
prisingly natural. So does the sturdy and capacious boat;
and the relationship of the three figures in space is a
further sign of Duccio's striving for more lifelike effects.

66. REMBRANDT: *Christ in the Storm on the Sea of Galilee*

< PRECEDING PAGE

66. Christ in the Storm on the Sea of Galilee
BY REMBRANDT 1606–1669 *Dutch School*
Isabella Stewart Gardner Museum, Boston

And behold, there arose a great storm on the sea, so that the boat was covered by the waves; but he was asleep. So they came and woke him, saying, "Lord, save us! we are perishing!" MATTHEW 8:24–25

MUCH OF REMBRANDT'S early work shows the vigorous movement and the dramatic contrasts we think of as the more obvious qualities of the Baroque style. In this picture of 1633, painted soon after his arrival in Amsterdam, he comes close to Rubens: the forces of wind and water are clashing so fiercely that they almost seem to merge into one, crushing the boat between them. For the Dutch, who as lowland dwellers knew the threat of the sea from personal experience, this scene had a direct bearing on their daily lives; they could easily imagine themselves in the same boat with Christ, since Rembrandt has painted a fishing boat of the kind actually in use at that time.

67.　CARAVAGGIO: *The Calling of Matthew*

< PRECEDING PAGE

67. The Calling of Matthew (detail)
BY CARAVAGGIO 1573–1610 *Italian School*
S. Luigi dei Francesi, Rome

Now as Jesus passed on from there, he saw a man named Matthew sitting in the tax-collector's place, and said to him, "Follow me." And he arose and followed him. MATTHEW 9:9

CARAVAGGIO WAS THE LAST in the succession of supremely great Italian masters whose impact changed the course of art throughout Europe. He is the chief founder of Baroque painting, who inspired artists as diverse as Rembrandt and Rubens, Georges de La Tour and Luca Giordano. Caravaggio's canvases, despite their down-to-earth realism, are filled with deep religious feeling, conveyed through their sharply focused, expressive lighting. In our picture, Christ appears as a humble man of the people in contrast to the colorfully dressed group on the left. His commanding gesture, however, is borrowed directly from Michelangelo's *God Creating Adam* (plate 2).

68.   GIOVANNI DI PAOLO: *The Head of the Baptist is Brought Before Herod*

< PRECEDING PAGE

68. The Head of the Baptist is Brought Before Herod
BY GIOVANNI DI PAOLO c.1403–1482/83
Italian School, The Art Institute of Chicago
   (Mr. and Mrs. Martin A. Ryerson Collection)

But sending an executioner. . . . he beheaded him in the
prison, and brought his head on a dish. MARK 6:27–28

IN THE MIDST of the Early Renaissance, Giovanni di Paolo
of Siena was an oddly conservative artist who remained
faithful to the Gothic style of his youth throughout his
long and prolific career. Although our picture was painted
about the same time as the Arezzo frescoes of Piero della
Francesca (plate 39), it seems far more akin to such
earlier works as Gentile da Fabriano's *Adoration of the
Magi* (plate 57), with its ornate costumes, its smoothly
curving loops of drapery, and its gay, decorative colors.
There is a fairy-tale charm about the scene that belies the
gruesome character of the subject; instead of sharing the
horror of Herod and his table companions, we find ourselves marveling at the faithful halo that accompanies the
severed head of the Saint.

69.   DUCCIO: *The Transfiguration*

< PRECEDING PAGE

69. The Transfiguration
BY DUCCIO c.1255–1319 *Italian School*
National Gallery, London

Now after six days Jesus took Peter, James and John, and led them up a high mountain off by themselves, and was transfigured before them. MARK 9:1

IN COMPARING THE FIGURE of Christ in this panel with those in the same artist's *Temptation* and the *Calling of the Apostles Peter and Andrew* (plates 63, 65), we notice that here the Savior's garments are shaded in gold, to differentiate Him from the other figures (Moses and Elias beside him, Peter, John, and James below). This traditional way of visualizing the Divine nature of Christ appears to his disciples for the first time as God rather than man, with his face radiant as the sun and his garments white as the light. Elias, on the Savior's right, wears the camel's-hair cloak of John the Baptist, for in speaking to his disciples after the Transfiguration, Christ will reveal to them that John *was* Elias who had come again as prophesied but had gone unrecognized.

70.   MASACCIO: *The Tribute Money*

< PRECEDING PAGE

70. The Tribute Money (detail)

BY MASACCIO 1401–1428 *Italian School*

Brancacci Chapel, Church of the Carmine, Florence

"But that we may not give offense to them, go to the sea and cast a hook, and take the first fish that comes up. And opening its mouth thou wilt find a stater; take that and give it to them for me and for thee." MATTHEW 17:26

THE CYCLE FROM WHICH THIS DETAIL is taken represents the most important work of the youthful genius who created the Early Renaissance style in Florentine painting. His heavily cloaked figures have all the solidity and weight of Giotto's, but Masaccio also knew how to endow them with vigorous, well-articulated bodies beneath the garments, and with strongly differentiated, individual personalities. Moreover, he has placed them in a real landscape, full of light and atmosphere and extending as far as the eye can reach, while Giotto had been content with a shallow foreground stage barely deep enough to hold his figures (see Giotto's *Flight into Egypt,* plate 58).

71.   REMBRANDT: *The Woman Taken in Adultery*

< PRECEDING PAGE

71. The Woman Taken in Adultery
BY REMBRANDT 1606–1669 *Dutch School*
National Gallery, London

Now the Scribes and Pharisees brought a woman caught in adultery, and setting her in the midst, said to him, "Master, this woman has just now been caught in adultery." JOHN 8:3–4

THE DRAMATIC BEAM OF LIGHT that illuminates the main figures against a vast, mysterious background space still relates this picture of 1644 to the Baroque phase of Rembrandt's career (plates 32, 47, 66). But the violent movement so characteristic of his earlier work has already abated here, and the jewellike colors are taking on the mysterious golden glow of the artist's paintings of the 1650s and 1660s (see especially *Peter Denying his Master,* plate 78).

72. GEERTGEN TOT SINT JINS: *The Raising of Lazarus*

< PRECEDING PAGE

72. The Raising of Lazarus
BY GEERTGEN TOT SINT JANS c.1465–1490/95
Dutch School, The Louvre, Paris

*When he had said this, he cried out with a loud voice,
"Lazarus, come forth!" And at once he who had been
dead came forth, bound feet and hands with bandages, and
his face was tied up with a cloth.* JOHN 11:43–44

LITTLE IS KNOWN of this early Dutch artist beyond the fact
that he spent his brief career in Haarlem and that he died
young. Like other Netherlandish painters of his time, he
must have been linked, directly or indirectly, with the
tradition stemming from Rogier van der Weyden; the spa-
cious, softly hued landscape in our picture recalls Dieric
Bouts (plate 40), as do the colorful costumes of some of
the bystanders (plates 8, 22). Yet Geertgen has one de-
cisive quality of his own that endears him especially to
modern eyes: a peculiar sense of the geometry of natural
shapes, which leads him to emphasize the basic egg shape
of the head and to design drapery, architecture, and even
landscape in terms of smooth, clean planes meeting at
precise angles.

73. GIOTTO: *Christ's Entry into Jerusalem*

< PRECEDING PAGE

73. Christ's Entry into Jerusalem
BY GIOTTO 1266?–1337 *Italian School*
Arena Chapel, Padua

So the disciples went and did as Jesus had directed them. And they brought the ass . . . and made him sit thereon. And most of the crowd spread their cloaks upon the road, while others were cutting branches from the trees, and strewing them on the road. MATTHEW 21:6–8

THE DRAMATIC SIMPLICITY of Giotto's art is again evident in this scene as it was in his *Flight into Egypt* (plate 58). He retains the details demanded by the scriptural text— the spreading of garments in Christ's path, the cutting down and strewing of tree branches—yet condenses the narrative into three main elements: Christ in the center, the massive group of disciples behind him, and the welcoming throng at the city gate. The entire action takes place in the immediate foreground, and by reducing the physical setting of the event to a minimum, Giotto further centers all our attention upon the figures.

74. EL GRECO: *Christ Driving the Money-Changers from the Temple*

< PRECEDING PAGE

74. Christ Driving the Money-Changers from the
     Temple (detail)
BY EL GRECO 1541–1614 *Spanish School*
National Gallery, London

And Jesus entered the temple of God, and cast out all
those who were selling and buying in the temple, and he
overturned the tables of the money-changers and the seat
of those who sold the doves. MATTHEW 21:12

THIS, CHRIST'S FIRST ACT upon entering Jerusalem, was a
favorite subject of El Greco. The version reproduced here
dates from his mature years; the elongated figures, the
ecstatic gestures, the flickering light recall his *Adoration*
of the Shepherds (plate 55). In the architectural setting,
with its heavy columns and walls, we may find an echo of
similar settings El Greco had seen in Venice some twenty
years before, although the space in our picture is as irra-
tional (measured by Renaissance standards) as that in the
Adoration. Indeed, perhaps the chief purpose of the temple
walls is to display the two marble reliefs, whose subjects,
however sketchily painted, are of great significance: on
the left the Expulsion from Paradise, the Old Testament
analogue of Christ's own sacrificial death.

75. LEONARDO DA VINCI: *The Last Supper*

< PRECEDING PAGE

75. The Last Supper

BY LEONARDO DA VINCI 1452–1519 *Italian School*

Sta. Maria delle Grazie, Milan

But he answered and said, "He who dips his hand into the dish with me, he will betray me." MATTHEW 26:23

DESPITE THE FACT that for the past four centuries the *Last Supper* has, physically, been a mere shadow of its original self, Leonardo's masterpiece remains one of the great classics of Christian art. It would take a survey not only of the artist's own copious studies for the picture but of earlier representations of the subject, to reach a full understanding of what Leonardo has achieved here. The secret of his success, surely, is balance: balance between spatial depth and surface design; between the human significance of the event, as displayed in the impetuous psychological reactions of the individual Apostles, and its ritual, symbolic meaning, reflected in the serene image of Christ and the formal symmetry of the composition. This complete harmony of the real and ideal embodies the highest aims of Renaissance art.

76. EL GRECO: *Christ on the Mount of Olives*

< PRECEDING PAGE

76. Christ on the Mount of Olives (detail)
BY EL GRECO 1541–1614 *Spanish School*
National Gallery, London

*And there appeared to him an angel from heaven to
strengthen him. And falling into an agony he prayed the
more earnestly. And his sweat became as drops of blood
running down upon the ground.* LUKE 22:43–44

THIS WORK OF EL GRECO'S late years is as magnificently
subjective and visionary as his *Adoration* (plate 55). All
the forms—whether rocks, clouds, or human bodies—are
of a strange transparency, filled with an iridescent glow
from within; they overlap, interpenetrate (note the cocoon-
like clouds that frame the sleeping Apostles), merge into
a rhythmic pattern that fills the entire canvas. Any comparison with the world of everyday experience is excluded
here: El Greco, as it were, challenges us to accept or reject
the visual poetry of his picture as an integrated whole that
cannot be broken down into its component parts.

77. GIOTTO: *The Taking of Christ*

< PRECEDING PAGE

77. The Taking of Christ

BY GIOTTO 1266?–1337 *Italian School*

Arena Chapel, Padua

Now his betrayer had given them a sign, saying, "Whom-ever I kiss, that is he; lay hold of him." And he went straight up to Jesus and said, "Hail, Rabbi!" and kissed him. MATTHEW 26:48–49

THE MOST MEMORABLE QUALITY of this scene is its grave matter-of-factness. For Giotto, the nocturnal scene holds no interest apart from the human drama; the two flaming torches have no effect upon the illumination of the picture. On the other hand, we become aware immediately of the forest of spears and clubs, all of them converging upon the Savior who endures the kiss of Judas. There is a moving contrast between the gentle, submissive figure of Christ and the dense crowd around him, their features distorted with evil passion. Even Peter, cutting off the ear of Mal-chus, partakes of this world of violence that is closing in upon the Prince of Peace.

78.　REMBRANDT: *Peter Denying His Master*

< PRECEDING PAGE

78. Peter Denying His Master (detail)
BY REMBRANDT 1606–1669 *Dutch School*
Rijksmuseum, Amsterdam

The maid, who was portress, said therefore to Peter, "Art thou also one of this man's disciples?" He said, "I am not." Now the servants and attendants were standing at a coal fire and warming themselves, for it was cold. And Peter also was with them, standing and warming himself. JOHN 18:17–18

THE MOST MEMORABLE CANVASES of Rembrandt's old age, such as this one or the *David Playing the Harp before Saul* (plate 36), are those devoted to the frailty of the human spirit. It is not the action itself but the state of the soul from which it springs that the artist explores in these pictures. The light of the candle held by the maid throws into relief the infinite sadness of the disciple who denies his master as Christ in the background turns toward him with a compassionate glance. Only an artist of consummate human insight could have endowed the scene with such a wealth of expressive meaning.

79. TINTORETTO: *Christ Before Pilate*

< PRECEDING PAGE

79. Christ Before Pilate (detail)

BY TINTORETTO 1518–1594 *Italian School*

Scuola di San Rocco, Venice

Now Pilate, seeing that he was doing no good, but rather that a riot was breaking out, took water and washed his hands in sight of the crowd, saying, "I am innocent of the blood of this just man; see to it yourselves." MATTHEW 27:24

WHEN THE YOUNG EL GRECO arrived in Venice from his native Crete, the painter who impressed him most was Tintoretto, then at the height of his power. The link between the two is readily seen if we compare this picture with El Greco's *Christ Driving the Money-Changers from the Temple* (plate 74), not only in the architectural setting but in the elongated, twisting figures and the flickering, unsteady light. The slender, motionless Christ of Tintoretto's canvas, cloaked in white, the color of innocence, stands out unforgettable against the turmoil around him.

80.   BOSCH: *The Crowning of Thorns*

< PRECEDING PAGE

80. The Crowning of Thorns

BY HIERONYMUS BOSCH 1450/60–1516

Flemish School, National Gallery, London

And plaiting a crown of thorns, they put it upon his head, and a reed into his right hand; and bending the knee before him they mocked him, saying, "Hail, King of the Jews!"
MATTHEW 27:29

EVEN THOUGH BOSCH was a Dutch painter more than half a century older than Tintoretto, he too has placed a white-robed, motionless Christ in the midst of a circle of viciously passionate torturers. These four figures, one suspects, are intended to have a significance beyond the context of this particular scene: they are differentiated from each other with great care, and each carries some symbol or attribute to identify his role. Unfortunately, we no longer know the meaning of all of these signs, but the crescent-and-star on the headdress of the old man on the lower left obviously stands for Mohammedanism (or heresy in general) and the oak leaves on the hat of the soldier in the opposite corner are, in all probability, a heathen emblem. The four heads thus represent sin-ridden, unbelieving mankind as a whole, and the beholder is faced with the question, "Which of these is you?"

81. SIMONE MARTINI: *Christ Carrying the Cross*

< PRECEDING PAGE

81. Christ Carrying the Cross

BY SIMONE MARTINI 1285?–1344 *Italian School*

The Louvre, Paris

And bearing the cross for himself, he went forth to the place called the Skull, in Hebrew, Golgotha. JOHN 19:17

AMONG THE PAINTERS of Siena who arose in the wake of Duccio, Simone Martini was one of the most venturesome and individual. The figures in his narrative panels such as this one have something of the impressive bulk and weight of Giotto's, and the variety of facial expressions is greater than we find in the work of any earlier artist. The crowd includes many contemporary types, such as the group of soldiers behind Christ or the man who helps Him carry the cross. The view of Jerusalem, too, shows the architectural features of Medieval Italian towns. Our panel was, however, not painted in Siena but in Avignon, where Simone spent the last years of his life at the Papal Court.

82. EL GRECO: *The Disrobing of Christ*

< PRECEDING PAGE

82. The Disrobing of Christ

BY EL GRECO 1541–1614 *Spanish School*

Cathedral, Toledo, Spain

And when they had mocked him, they took the purple off him and put his own garments on him, and led him out to crucify him. MARK 15:20

THIS IS THE SCENE immediately preceding the Crucifixion: the executioners are about to divest Christ of the robe they had put on him earlier in mockery of His kingship. In the lower right-hand corner, a man is preparing the cross. Our picture, painted not long after El Greco's arrival in Toledo from Italy, still includes many realistic features that will disappear in the artist's later work (plates 55, 88). Yet the steeply rising ground, the oddly condensed space, and above all the centering of the entire composition on the huge, brilliantly colored robe anticipate qualities of El Greco's most mature phase.

83.   VERONESE: *Calvary*

< PRECEDING PAGE

83. Calvary

BY PAOLO VERONESE 1528–1588 *Italian School*

The Louvre, Paris

And when they came to the place called the Skull, they crucified him there. LUKE 23:33

THE CRUCIFIXION, the central theme of Christian art, has yielded an almost infinite variety of visual interpretations through the centuries; the Savior on the cross could be shown as a hieratic symbol or as a human being in the agony of death; He could be isolated for devotional contemplation or placed among the crowd who, according to the scriptural account, witnessed the event. Veronese's version is quietly lyrical rather than dramatic. It depicts the moment after Christ's death—darkness is falling over the earth, the idle spectators have departed, St. John and the women in the foreground are for the moment preoccupied with the fainting Virgin Mary; and the ladder raised against the cross indicates that preparations are under way to take down the body of the Savior.

84. REMBRANDT: *The Descent from the Cross*

< PRECEDING PAGE

84. The Descent from the Cross

BY REMBRANDT 1606–1669 *Dutch School*

Pinakothek, Munich

And behold, there was a man named Joseph . . . of Arima-
thea, a town of Judea, who was himself looking for the
kingdom of God. He went to Pilate and asked for the body
of Jesus. And he took him down. LUKE 23:50–53

REMBRANDT PAINTED THIS PICTURE in 1633, the year he
did the *Christ in the Storm on the Sea of Galilee* (plate
66). There is indeed a strong similarity of style between
the two, despite the contrasting subject matter. Here as
before the artist trains a brilliant beam of light upon the
central action, against a dark background of bluish and
greenish gray. This subdued range of colors lends particular force to the sudden flash of brightness: in our picture,
it also emphasizes the red bloodstains on the wood of the
cross. To satisfy his desire for dramatic action, so strong
in all the works of the 1630s, Rembrandt has visualized the
lowering of the Savior's body as a strained, precarious
operation awkwardly performed: perhaps it is this awk-
wardness that makes the scene so touching.

85.   EL GRECO: *The Dead Christ in the Arms of God the Father*

< PRECEDING PAGE

85. The Dead Christ in the Arms of God the Father
BY EL GRECO 1541–1614 *Spanish School*
The Prado, Madrid

*He who has not spared even his own Son but has delivered
him for us all, how can he fail to grant us also all things
with him?* ROMANS 8:32

THERE IS NO SCRIPTURAL PASSAGE which this scene may be
said to illustrate. The image of the dead Christ supported
by God the Father, with the dove of the Holy Spirit hover-
ing above, was created in the later Middle Ages as a striking visual summary of the Passion and its meaning for
mankind. Its sources are Northern European rather than
Italian, and El Greco's impressive composition is based
on a woodcut by Albrecht Dürer, even though he painted
it very soon after his arrival in Spain. His style here is
more completely Italian than in any of his subsequent
works: note especially the beautiful, solidly modeled body
of Christ, a last echo of the heroic forms of Michelangelo.

86.   GIOTTO: *The Lamentation Over Christ*

< PRECEDING PAGE

86. The Lamentation Over Christ

BY GIOTTO 1266?–1337 *Italian School*

Arena Chapel, Padua

At nightfall, weeping enters in; but with the dawn, rejoic-ing. PSALMS 29:6

THIS SCENE, TOO, is not described in the Gospels but freely interpolated between the Descent from the Cross and the Entombment. Yet we can well understand why it was so frequently represented in Medieval and Renaissance art, for it permitted the artist to explore the full range of ex-pressions of grief unhampered by narrative requirements. Giotto's version, one of the earliest, is also among the greatest, and the most famous single scene from his Paduan cycle. His severe, simple shapes, and the measured rhythm of the composition, only serve to heighten the emotional impact of these mourners.

87.   VAN DER WEYDEN: *The Entombment*

< PRECEDING PAGE

87. The Entombment

BY ROGIER VAN DER WEYDEN 1399/1400–1464

Flemish School, Uffizi Gallery, Florence

And Joseph . . . laid him in a tomb which had been hewn out of a rock. Then he rolled a stone to the entrance of the tomb. But Mary Magdalene and Mary the mother of Joseph were looking on and saw where he was laid. MARK 15:46–47

EVEN THOUGH ITS SUBJECT implies action, Rogier's *Entombment* is very much more passive in spirit than Giotto's *Lamentation.* The body of Christ, rigid and angular as if carved out of wood, is being exhibited to Mary Magdalene —and to us—like an effigy for pious contemplation, and the strict symmetry of the central group of figures further emphasizes their formal, ceremonial character. The gestures, too, are muted; our emotional sympathy is invited solely by the grief-stricken glances. Yet their silent appeal is so moving that we find ourselves sharing the sorrow of these men and women more intimately than we are permitted to in Giotto's picture.

88. EL GRECO: *The Resurrection*

< PRECEDING PAGE

88. The Resurrection

BY EL GRECO 1541–1614 *Spanish School*

The Prado, Madrid

And for fear of him the guards were terrified, and became like dead men. But the angel spoke and said to the women. . . . "He is not here, for he has risen." MATTHEW 28:4–6

THIS WORK, painted some thirty years after the *Dead Christ in the Arms of God the Father,* shows the ecstatic late style of El Greco even more strikingly than does the *Adoration* (plate 55). The triumphant Risen Christ soars victoriously above the guardians of the tomb, the defeated forces of evil, as if propelled by some tremendous explosive force. Here, the artist seems to tell us, is a miracle even greater than that of the birth of the Savior—a miracle so overpowering that it must be hailed by the very men who had struggled against it. Although earthbound, they, too, share in the undulating upward movement that fills the entire canvas. This fervent rhythm, rather than the narrative as such, is El Greco's only concern during the final years of his life. Hence his sovereign disregard for the setting of the scene; even the tomb itself has disappeared behind the screen of interwoven limbs.

89.   SCHOOL OF ORCAGNA: *The Three Marys at the Tomb*

< PRECEDING PAGE

89. The Three Marys at the Tomb

BY SCHOOL OF ORCAGNA (14th century)

Italian School, National Gallery, London

And when the Sabbath was past, Mary Magdalene, Mary the mother of James, and Salome, bought spices, that they might go and anoint him. . . . And looking up they saw that the stone had been rolled back, for it was very large. MARK 16:1, 4

THE CLEAR COLORS and the ample use of gold relate this panel to such earlier masters as Duccio and Simone Martini (plates 63, 81). Actually, it is by a Florentine, a charming but modest painter in the wake of Orcagna, and thus reflects the art of Giotto as well. The simple clarity of the picture space and the tangible, rounded quality of the figures derive from that source. There is, however, also a new element, characteristic of the late years of the fourteenth century: the interest in direct observation that has caused our artist to cover the foreground with precisely rendered small plants and flowers. This spring meadow still has some of the decorative regularity of a tapestry pattern but it nevertheless betrays an awareness of nature that will find more complete expression in the years to come.

90.   TITIAN: *Noli Me Tangere*

< PRECEDING PAGE

90. Noli Me Tangere
BY TITIAN 1477?–1576 *Italian School*
National Gallery, London

*Jesus said to her, "Do not touch me, for I have not yet
ascended to my Father."* JOHN 20:17

THE FLOWER CARPET of the *Three Marys* may be viewed
as the first harbinger of a development that was to reach
its highest point a century and a half later in the magnificent landscape vistas of the Venetian High Renaissance.
To Titian, landscape is no longer a mere setting, something to be added to a figure composition; in pictures such
as ours, the landscape encloses—and almost dominates—
the figures. It is this wonderfully atmospheric view of the
countryside, aglow with the last rays of the setting sun,
that determines the mood of the picture; a mood singularly
gentle and poetic, as befits the encounter between Mary
Magdalene and the gardener who is the Risen Christ.

91. REMBRANDT: *Christ at Emmaus*

< PRECEDING PAGE

91. Christ at Emmaus

BY REMBRANDT 1606–1669 *Dutch School*

The Louvre, Paris

And it came to pass when he reclined at table with them, that he took the bread and blessed and broke and began handing it to them. And their eyes were opened, and they recognized him. LUKE 24:30–31

THE TWO DISCIPLES encountering the Risen Christ at Emmaus is a subject painted more than once by Rembrandt at various stages of his development. Our version, the best known and most mature, no longer stresses the drama of recognition but envelopes the figures in a lyrical mood rather like that of Titian's *Noli Me Tangere*. Here, as in so many of his later works, Rembrandt is concerned with inward rather than outward experience; the disciples recognize the Lord as he breaks the bread, and Rembrandt's composition suggests what went on in their minds: the scene recalls to them (and to us) the Last Supper, and its full meaning is revealed only when they become aware that they are once again at the Lord's table.

92.　MANTEGNA: *The Ascension*

$<$ PRECEDING PAGE

92. The Ascension

BY ANDREA MANTEGNA 1431–1506 *Italian School*
Uffizi Gallery, Florence

Now he led them out towards Bethany, and he lifted up his hands and blessed them. And it came to pass as he blessed them, that he parted from them and was carried up into heaven. LUKE 24:50–51

OF ALL THE GREAT MASTERS of the Italian Early Renaissance, Mantegna had the strongest sense of drama. And he knew better than any of his contemporaries how to utilize the newly gained knowledge of scientific perspective so as to heighten the expressive effect of his compositions. The *Ascension* is a splendid example of this: by placing the horizon close to the bottom edge of the panel, Mantegna forces us to view the scene from an eye-level a good deal lower than that of the figures in the foreground, giving us, as it were, a worm's-eye view of the scene. As a result, we share the steep upward glances of Mary and the Apostles, and the gap between them and Christ, between earth and heaven, becomes a truly memorable experience.

93.   EL GRECO: *The Pentecost*

< PRECEDING PAGE

93. The Pentecost

BY EL GRECO 1541–1614 *Spanish School*

The Prado, Madrid

And there appeared to them parted tongues as of fire,
which settled upon each of them. And they were all filled
with the Holy Spirit and began to speak in foreign tongues,
even as the Holy Spirit prompted them to speak. ACTS 2:3–4

IF WE HAD TO CHOOSE the subject most completely suited
to the late style of El Greco, we should have to insist on
the *Pentecost*. Here the uniting of all participants in a
common ecstasy of spiritual joy is the very essence of the
theme, and the flamelike movements of light and color
culminate in the actual tongues of flame marking the
Descent of the Holy Ghost. Our canvas has the same tall,
narrow format and the same arched top as the *Resurrection* (plate 88); both, we may surmise, formed the upper
part of large altarpieces. They must have been meant, then,
to be viewed from below, a circumstance that could only
increase their emotional impact.

94. DÜRER: *The Four Apostles*

< PRECEDING PAGE

94. The Four Apostles

BY ALBRECHT DÜRER 1471–1528 *German School*

Pinakothek, Munich

And he himself gave some men as apostles . . . for building up the body of Christ. EPHESIANS 4:11–12

SOON AFTER 1500, the influence of Italian Renaissance art made itself felt more and more strongly north of the Alps, where it intermingled with (and finally replaced) the tradition stemming from Rogier van der Weyden. Dürer was in the forefront of this movement; he had been to Venice twice in his younger years, and it was there that he first became acquainted with figures of the monumental simplicity of his own *Four Apostles.* The two panels, originally planned as the wings of an altar, are his last and greatest achievement in painting, completed only two years before his death. In fact, they may be said to be a kind of artistic last will and testament, since Dürer presented them to his home town of Nuremberg as an embodiment of his most cherished beliefs.

95. CARAVAGGIO: *The Conversion of Paul*

< PRECEDING PAGE

95. The Conversion of Paul

BY CARAVAGGIO 1573–1610 *Italian School*

Sta. Maria del Popolo, Rome

Suddenly a light from heaven shone round about him; and falling to the ground, he heard a voice saying to him, "Saul, Saul, why dost thou persecute me?" ACTS 9:3–4

THE REVOLUTIONARY, down-to-earth realism of Caravaggio's religious paintings is as strikingly present in this canvas as in his *Calling of Matthew* (plate 67). Contrary to traditional custom, he shows Paul not at the head of a column of armed men but as a simple soldier himself, whose conversion is witnessed only by the horse and the aged groom. His fall has been dramatized through the extreme foreshortening of his body and the exceptionally low eye-level of the beholder, which makes the riderless horse loom so tall that it almost fills the upper half of the picture. There is even less movement here than in the *Matthew,* but for that very reason we become aware of the vital role of the light as the carrier of inner experience to a greater degree than ever before.